Contents

The Hope Slide

In loving memory of my father
who taught me how to tell a story

Frederick Campbell MacLeod

1907-1990

Acknowledgements

This play was written with the generous support of the Canada Council. As always I wish to thank Urjo Kareda and my many friends at the Tarragon for their support. I also want to thank Theatre Columbus, Bill Lane, Roy Surette, Patrick McDonald and Sean Breaugh. And Bruce Armstrong (Kootenay tour guide), Ken Garnhum (builder of monuments) and Don Hannah (sorter of debris). Most importantly I want to thank Glynis Leyshon, Sarah Orenstein and Leslie Jones for everything but especially for helping to create Irene.

Preface

From growing up in North Vancouver in the 1960s, I remember the sound of the nine o'clock gun promptly punctuating lazy summer evenings. I remember the thrill of traveling on the Hope-Princeton highway shortly after the Hope Slide turned a green B.C. valley into a surreal moonscape of raw earth and jagged boulders. And I remember staring, with giggles and guilty interest, at newspaper pictures of shockingly naked Doukhobor women.

All those disconnected, half-forgotten memories came back to haunt me while I was working on the premiere of Joan MacLeod's extraordinary new drama, *The Hope Slide*. Because I had already directed two of Joan's earlier plays—*Amigo's Blue Guitar* and *Toronto, Mississippi*—the power and precise beauty of her work came as no surprise to me. Again and again during the rehearsal period I was awed by Joan MacLeod's poetic gift for lifting memories of the 'ordinary', the 'everyday', and making them live with mythic clarity.

Brought together by Urjo Kareda at the Tarragon Theatre, all of us involved in mounting *The Hope Slide* were enticed by the obvious challenges that the script presented. Unlike her earlier monologue, *Jewel*, which observed a unity of time and place, Joan wanted to implode the dramatic unities in *The Hope Slide*. The work explores three profoundly different realities: a past, a present and an entirely poetic world of dramatic

11

'testaments.' Each is vital to the other but not in an immediately apparent way. It is only as the play unfolds that the audience gradually becomes aware of the web of ideas and images that connect, and finally unite, all three realities.

Theatrically, we came to believe that each of these realities required an entirely different style of presentation. The 'now' seemed to be contained and enclosed, while the 'past' seemed to explode with youthful energy. The 'testaments' were inherently dramatic and seemed to cry out for a bold, theatrical treatment. This approach obviously placed huge demands on the solo-actor, and the original production owed much to the prodigious talents and remarkable intelligence of Sarah Orenstein.

The central reality or 'now' of the play lies in the story of Irene Dickson, a middle-aged actress who is touring central B.C. with a one-woman show about the Doukhobors. *The Hope Slide* begins with Irene in deep distress. Driven from the warmth of a billeted bed, she sits alone in a living-room and begins to grapple with her fears. She wonders why hope 'has become a threatened species, with bowed head and awkward feet, cold and trembling. Terrified.'

During this night of self-examination Joan MacLeod has Irene return to her past; to a time both literally and figuratively before the Hope Slide occurred. This past represents the play's second reality, and it is dominated by one of the most unforgettable creations in contemporary drama. The young Irene is vital, fierce, wickedly funny and achingly vulnerable. Irene is an awkward outsider whose passionate need to belong leads her to an obsessive love for the rebellious Doukhobor community. Like her soul-mate, Walter, young Irene is an idealist whose dream is that together they will build a perfect city, a place protected from all possible danger.

Woven into the worlds of past and present are the testaments that constitute the play's third reality. There are three such testaments: poetic, richly imagistic monologues that bring to life the distinct voices of three Doukhobor martyrs.

Only gradually do we come to understand that these monologues are the one-woman show that the older Irene is touring. We also come to understand, as does Irene herself, that by retelling these testaments written by three people at the moment of their death, she is keeping their stories alive. As an artist she is bearing witness to the bravery and beauty of their individual existences.

The conclusion of *The Hope Slide* is a highly charged, deeply felt response to a horror that faces all of us. Joan rewrites the play's separate realities and allows the past to inform Irene's present and to shape her future.

We learn in language as spare and unsentimental as a Doukhobor hymn that Walter has died of AIDS. Like so many of our best and brightest, he is gone, and in her pain Irene has buried not only Walter, but Hope as well.

But the hard journey of self-discovery that Irene makes in the play leads her back to Hope and to action, to protest in the manner of her beloved Doukhobors.

The Hope Slide invites us all to protest the horror of the dark plague that is robbing us of our best and brightest. Above all it invites us to share their stories, to bear witness to their bravery, and to never, never forget.

—Glynis Leyshon

The Hope Slide was first presented by the Tarragon Theatre, Toronto, in March 1992, with the following:

IRENE . . . . .Sarah Orenstein

Director: Glynis Leyshon
Set & Costume Designer: Sean Breaugh
Lighting Designer: W.E. Gosling

The Hope Slide takes place during one night in the Kootenays, a remote and mountainous area four hundred miles east of Vancouver, in 1990. During this night Irene travels from 1962 to 1967, from North Vancouver to the Doukhobor prison outside the town of Hope, from the turbulent Kootenays of the early sixties to the other side of Hope where a mountain collapsed in 1965.

The play is in one act. There is no intermission.

Lights up on the adult IRENE, thirty-seven years old. It is the middle of the night, in the Kootenays, January 1990. IRENE is sitting in a comfortable chair, wrapped up in a quilt.

My first version of girlie pictures were these grainy photographs of Doukhobor women that my brother cut out of the *Vancouver Sun* and kept in a drawer behind his socks. This long line of big bums and kerchiefs. We were United Church so all this was pretty exotic, sexy as hell. When I was very little I thought Doukhobor meant untidy but then I started thinking they were true heroes because they didn't send their kids to school and when they were really pissed off they burnt down the school altogether. School was always a horrible place for me. My marks were terrible; I had the attention span of a flea.

Wanna play teenager? This used to be my favourite game. We'd roll up our skirts, smoke cherry bark and run around kissing one another. Wanna play Teenage Doukhobor? It's the same idea only the one who's it has to take off her pants. I was a very religious child. I used to light Kleenexes on fire and pray that Elvis would come, come to my house for supper. My parents would be out and all our furniture would be different.

In the seventies my friend Walter and I lived communally in the country and at first we attempted to organize our community on Doukhobor philosophy. We would have a meeting every Sunday, we would share household chores, men and women side by side, and any money made outside our quarter section would go into a communal kitty. The system began to break down when none of us wanted to work at regular jobs, in fact none of us wanted to work period. Walter's definition of housework included braiding his hair. Walter was also completely in love with this really obnoxious guy called Peter who was one of our house-mates. This divided us further. Then there was this poor cat who froze to death in a well, who later showed up as a shoulder bag and beret. This was a simpler time, a hopeful time. I was working with puppets—everyone was working with puppets—I still bought all my footwear at the House of Clogs.

January 1990 and I am travelling through Doukhobor country, through the Kootenays. I am a full-fledged actor, I am an actor on tour, solo, bringing my own one-woman show to small places—three voices for the price of one. The characters I play were real people, ghosts I have stolen and made speak. Doukhobors. These are hard times and I am proud to be working. I am billeted with English teachers in interior towns; I eat surf 'n' turf with the head of the Chamber of Commerce. I arrive by bus, one a.m., exhausted and dying for a cigarette.

"I hope you like kids," a nervous mother asks while handing me a towel. "Absolutely," which is true. "Our little ones are up pretty early." I assure her that I am both an early riser and heavy sleeper—both lies.

I am exhausted but hyper, lying in a top bunk between Wayne Gretzky sheets—staring at a NO SMOKING sign the size of my head. I climb down the ladder and into their strange living-room. Through the window the great terror of mountains at night, a river beginning to freeze. I love my country—so beautiful and wild. My country is disappearing.

When the Doukhobors lived here they tried to create a heaven on earth. Forty of them living under one roof, families sleeping in long narrow beds, toe-to-toe. Everything was shared and because of this they prospered. As a girl they were heroes to me—model anarchists and rebels. Their expulsion from Russia I linked directly with my being expelled from junior high school. Truant officers were the bane of their existence—well, me too. I envied the Doukhobors many things but most of all I envied they had a community.

I have a community now, I have the theatre, and my community is under attack. The Minister of Revenue has just suggested a more "hands on" approach to funding the arts. I suggest we all lay our hands directly on the Minister of Revenue. But this is nothing compared to the real enemy. The moon is full, the stars close and sharp-looking, metallic, explosive. I prop open the sliding glass door so that I can sneak a cigarette. The air is very cold and clean. I am tired and I realize stupidly that I am down here because I am afraid to sleep, for the first time in years I am afraid of the dark. No more. No more funerals. Although I know many young men who look ahead with remarkable bravery, for many of my friends hope has become a threatened species, with a bowed head and awkward feet, cold and trembling. Terrified.

IRENE is fifteen, and, at first glance, conservatively dressed. She is wearing a scarf knotted at the side of her neck, a large locket, a cardigan that is on backwards. Her skirt is inside out. Her socks are worn over her shoes. She is standing behind a table. On the table is a loaf of bread, a cellar of salt, and a clear pitcher of water. IRENE is delivering her Social Studies project on the Doukhobors to her grade nine class, showing slides of the Doukhobors and project props throughout.

My name is Irene Dickson, Division Three, Grade Nine. My project is called The Doukhobors: Friend or Foe? I wish to thank the Audio-Visual Club for use of the overhead projector, although I would like to take this opportunity to point out that it's not as if they personally own the equipment, it's supposed to be for our use but I do digress. My project contains many interesting elements but no hand-outs. Let us begin. The Doukhobors: Friend or Foe?

The Doukhobors came to be around the middle of the eighteenth century, utopian peasants whose beliefs went back to a bunch of groups that parted company with the Orthodox Church in Holy Russia as part of the Great Schism.

The Doukhobors settled by the Molochnaya River, the Milky Waters and, depending on the mood of the current Tsar and their neighbours, lived as Martyrs under terrible persecution or as Happy Communal Farmers. Their refusal to bear arms, i.e., fight and kill, and their refusal to register their marriages, births, deaths, etc. and so forth meant they were in extreme trouble more often than not. And so ... on January 20th, 1899, the steamer the *Lake Huron* arrived in

Halifax with the first of four shiploads of passengers.
All in all seven thousand four hundred and twenty-
seven Doukhobors came to Canada which was the
majority of their numbers. The second boatload
contained seven hundred children with Count Sergei
Tolstoy, son of the extremely famous writer, in charge.
Count Leo Tolstoy, the writer to whom I just referred,
now dead of course, nominated the Doukhobors for
the Nobel Peace Prize. They didn't win but this was still
a high honour to be nominated. With the royalties
from his last novel, *Resurrection,* and with help from the
Quakers, as in porridge, the Doukhobor's passage from
Russia to Canada was made. Although he himself was
extremely wealthy Leo Tolstoy had spent a large
portion of his life dreaming of *anarchist Christian
peasants* and when he heard of the Doukhobors he felt
he had hit the nail on the head. The Halifax paper
described the new immigrants as follows: "People of
the purest Russian type, large and strong, men and
women both being of magnificent physique with a
bright kindly sparkle to their eyes." I also want to add
that this is about the last nice thing I have found in the
newspapers about the Doukhobors during my research
which has been both personal and exhaustive and goes
right from the eighteenth century until 1967—i.e.,
now. I know you are all well aware that I did live with
the Doukhobors for a short time last year but that
experience is personal, untouchable and purely mine.

The Doukhobors settled in Saskatchewan and in
practically no time their communities were thriving.
The government says okay to no military service but
insists that the Doukhobors register their lands in
individual names which the Doukhobors will not do

because they share everything. So ... some Doukhobors stay in Saskatchewan and the rest go out to B.C. with their great leader Peter Veregin in charge.

Doukhobors are very different from say, the United Church—which is the faith my parents have forced on me, or the Catholics who I disagree with on several issues, i.e., everything—in that the Doukhobors have no icons, no fasts and no festivals, no churches and no priests. They are pacifists and refuse to bear arms for any cause. Their stories and beliefs are passed on orally through their psalms—the Living Book. Traditional schools and written law are not only stupid to them but terrifying. The only law is God's law and to bow before the laws of man is to unite with Satan. All teachers, of course, are instruments of the devil. The Sons of Freedom believed that higher education, i.e., junior high school included, quote—turns you into a truly insane animal. End quote.

Their only obvious symbols of faith are the loaf of bread, the cellar of salt and the jug of water. When I come into the meeting hall, into the sobranya, I recognize in each one of you the divine spark. And I bow.

IRENE bows to several individuals in the audience.

You're supposed to bow back. Your participation is an integral part of my project.

IRENE begins to sing.

"Fortunate is he who loves all living creatures
The pulse of creation beats dear to his heart
For whom all in nature is kindred and near
Man and bird, flower and tree, none to him stand apart."

1903. The first stirrings of the group called Svobodniki or Freedomite or Sons of Freedom. Sixty men, women and children wander from village to village, reminding their sisters and brothers to reject all material things: they nibble the leaves off young trees, eat the grass, they set their animals free and give any money they might have to the authorities. They believe absolutely that God will provide for them and to show their simplicity and innocence they "go in the manner of the first: Adam and Eve"—i.e. naked. I would like to point out that naked is innocent to them not dirty.

Alright grade nine. How many of you are wearing a wristwatch? If I had some dynamite I could show you a simple method for making a bomb using only your watch, a stick of dynamite and a little common sense. Making of bombs is what they call black work and in 1923 the first of many schools in B.C. was burnt to the ground. Burnings, like nudity, at first meant a return to simplicity and purity but now became a form of protest.

This black work was often spur of the moment, they would be gripped by a sudden and mad inspiration and, like myself, worked best without a plan.

Basically this is how it all works: you want me to send my kids to school and I say no because I know school is evil and that you are going to teach my children a load of crap. So. You have this early-morning raid of truant officers in my village and gather my children and take them to the government school in New Denver—as in the place where the Japanese were locked up during the war. I steal my kids back and just as a little insurance, I burn down the local school. A solution, a

simple solution. I also might set my own house on fire
just to show you I don't care about material things. If
my Doukhobor neighbours are getting a little too
greedy I might burn down their house too so that they
can get back to basics. If you have still missed the point
I might just take all my clothes off or blow up a bridge.
These are called the "upside down" days, demonstra-
tion to follow now. Because the RCMP, disguised as
Doukhobors—fat chance—infiltrated their meetings,
the leaders would wear their clothes in weird ways and
this meant reverse all statements I am telling you—i.e.,
(*slowly building to a frenzy*) ... If I am telling you to go
out and love your brother, your brother and our
principal Mr. Miller in particular, you know because my
shirt is on backwards that I really mean, *burn,* go on, do
it, light a fire under this school or perhaps under Mr.
Miller's house.

IRENE turns around, showing her backwards sweater.

Do not set fire to the offices of any newspapers. I
mean the *Vancouver Sun* in particular even though they
have made a blackout on Doukhobor matters, refuse to
publish our concerns.

IRENE begins to strip.

Keep your shirt on at all times. (*undoing her buttons*)
Do your buttons up, right to the top. Running around
naked? That is for children, that is for the little child.

She throws her sweater off and lights a match.

There are certain dead heroes that I wish to bring to
your attention! Harry Kootnikoff killed by fire, Paul

Podmorrow by hunger, Mary Kalmakoff swallowed by the earth!

I protest the death of these people! Heroes, victims, outlaws one and all! I protest we are sent home early and say prayers for Kennedy and Churchill and we are ignoring those dying in our own backyard. These are dark days, terrible times loom ahead! I protest the silence. "My heart is full of courage, brave to do something to make change, upheaval!"

These are the words of Paul Podmorrow who starved to death on a hunger strike!

> *IRENE's shirt is pulled up revealing a white cotton bra, her skirt is pulled down revealing waist-high underwear. A bell sounds, meaning 'stop.' IRENE continues to yell over the chaos.*

On behalf of him I call you to arms! I call you to fight goddamn you, fight goddamn you, fight goddamn you! *Fight!*

> *Blackout.*

> *The adult IRENE appears.*

I was always predicting the end of the world. The end of the world has been predicted a million times except in my case it almost happened. January 9, 1965. A wrinkle in the surface, part of the world heaved and buckled, let go for a moment and perhaps wanted to give in altogether, a mountain collapsed and threatened to bury a town just outside Vancouver. A mountain collapsed and threatened to bury the town of Hope. I didn't understand then that things are always changing, never steady. A shoreline shifts, rivers erupt, mountains fall. I thought death was only violent or accidental. Something for the very old and sick, the weak. I didn't understand then that people my own age might die, that young lives could be so painful.

Well. I understand it now.

IRENE lights a candle and speaks in the voice of Mary Kalmakoff, twenty-four years old, 1965.

I am pushing out against something. It is thin but tough—a strong piece of skin or good cotton sheet. And then I am through, above the buried car. I see my friends beside it—blood-spattered and still. I have special sight: I can see through the dark, the snow. It is three a.m., January, and we were driving through the mountains. Avalanche I am thinking now, this is an avalanche because snow has come right through the roof, filled up the convertible. Everything is still. I push through the rocks and snow and boulders of ice as though they are air. Travel through all this cold like a vein of boiling water. My skin should be scraped raw but it is clear, white and warm.

Stupid. I am pushing the wrong way, a stupid little mole that means to rise up and out of the mountain but instead aims for the heart, the centre of the earth. Then suddenly I am in the air again and tumbling down, the mountain tumbles with me and I understand what has happened, the mountain has cracked—its whole face and front side fallen, buried the road and the valley, left the mountain half-gone and naked. It seems fetal, ridiculous, unborn. I understand now too that I am dead and never to be found. Lost outside the town of Hope. Me. Mary Kalmakoff, twenty-four years old, unmarried. Employee of the Penticton Fruit Growers. Religion—Doukhobor.

> *IRENE is fifteen. A few months later. She is talking to her truant officer.*

First off I want it made perfectly clear that reporting to you, Miss Toye, a truant officer-slash-psychologist, is a complete violation of my rights and all I hold sacred and dear. The form in front of you was signed under duress, a condition of my being allowed back into school that I was forced to agree to. I was backed into a corner, the pen practically jammed into my hand. Although I am not against education per se I believe attendance should be voluntary.

My understanding, Miss Toye, is that I am to report to and talk to you, my truant officer-slash-warden, personally once a month and that if I am absent from school without a phone call and note from my mother or the queen mother or God himself then I am going to be expelled again. I agree to these conditions although it is with a heavy heart that I am agreeing. I also agree to keep my clothes on at all times, even in gym class I will wear my shorts over my stupid dress to avoid causing any further rioting amongst the members of my class. But although I am no longer allowed to protest publicly, I want you to know Mary Kalmakoff, Harry Kootnikoff and Paul Podmorrow are still heroes to me, unsung martyrs whose song I intend to keep alive come hell or high water.

These were real people who died an unjust and horrible death. How'd you like a mountain to fall on your head, Miss Toye? Or a bomb to explode in your lap? How'd you like to go on a hunger strike to get publicity but once you died nobody paid attention? The newspaper didn't even say it was sad. And this is absolutely the saddest thing that I think has ever happened but I do digress.

I would like you to write down right now that I, Irene Dickson, am absolutely thrilled to be back in school and that the idea of doing grade nine all over again is extremely exciting to me. I am turning over a new leaf, knuckling under; and disappointment is no longer a part of my life. I see this September as a new starting point on the rocky and difficult road of the life of *me*— Irene Dickson. You got all that?

What are you writing down? Everything on the form in front of you is totally true ... Except the part about my parents being divorced. It was an experiment I devised to see if people treat you any better if you come from a broken home. They don't. My parents get on like a house on fire, always have. The part about future occupation is true: dancer-slash-actress-slash-mayor of a great city. Present occupation: spirit wrestler. Meanness and forgiveness are growing inside me at an equal rate and creating an unholy war.

If you're going to write stuff down about me I think it is my right to see it ... Does it say there I have these theories?—i.e., last year I predicted North Van was going to slide into the ocean and settle like Atlantis under the Lions Gate Bridge. I also have several theories on hitchhiking, sex and friendship, drunken boys, the end of the world and, of course, the Doukhobors. Take your pick.

... Okay don't take your pick. Wanna talk about sex? No problem, anything goes here, I am an open book. Perhaps you are under the mistaken impression, along with the rest of this place, that Walter Dewitt is my boyfriend. That Walter Dewitt and I are doing it. Well, we're not. I do not see Walter in that way. He is my friend, my best friend, as a matter of fact, my only friend. You know Walter. He is very skinny and very bright, highly goofy. And like myself highly persecuted, my tribe. Walter and I believe friendship is the absolute highest state of being.

> *Pause.*

I like your hair. I believe women should have long hair, another one of my theories. In pre pre-historic times our hair was long so that babies, our babies could hold on while we ran through the trees being chased by God knows what. Babies are born knowing how to hold but now they've lost it and have to be taught. No. They come out knowing but then they forget and have to be taught. I don't know. But something has happened with regard to babies and their ability to hold on in this century.

I don't mean I don't ever think about sex. I think about it often. Perhaps constantly. Not the actual act of sex which is as yet unknown to me but I do think of my policies regarding sex: i.e., do everything but, you know, as many times as you want with whoever you want just *keep your hymen intact.* When I first learned of my hymen and the importance of keeping it untouched, in place, I imagined it this big shield I could hold out front and ward off guys with, rather like a Viking would have. It's a great word, hymen—hymn

and amen and hyena all rolled into one. This big
bouncy kangaroo thing that laughs its guts out. I mean
I know it isn't that and I know it isn't something that
you carry with a spear but I used to also worry that my
time will come, I will meet *him* and it will be perfect
and holy and wild but ... what if my hymen didn't
break? What if guys just sort of bounced off it? This
tough old piece of skin pulled tight as a drum, a bongo
drum barring the way to heaven.

What if it leaves men in pain? Pain is something they
cannot bear nearly as well as us. They also have a great
deal of trouble touching their own eyes.

Don't write that down! Just write down stuff like
I am knuckling under. I love that kind of crap. I am
knuckling under. I know, I know. Our time is up. Tell
me about it.

> *IRENE pulls up her scarf, bandit style, lights a match
> and speaks in the voice of a Doukhobor boy, Harry
> Kootnikoff, seventeen.*

Harry Kootnikoff, that is me and I am dead now.
Killed by fire. Poof ...

> *IRENE pulls down the scarf, blows out the match.*

This is the true story of what happened. I am with
four friends. The day is February 16, 1962. This is the
plan—we play crib for a while, then we go to the movie
in Trail, maybe meet a girl, have a good time, then
blow up the post office in Kinnaird at midnight and
call it a night. I am seventeen. I know dynamite as a
good friend since I am ten. I am the bomb-builder, the
man in charge, me. We go to a movie and while I watch

I have some of the bomb in the pocket of my coat and some of the bomb waiting in the back of our car. The Mounties pull us over, take the back seat right out and find nothing.

We know how to hide, us Doukhobors—hide dynamite, fuses, ourselves. When I am six *bang* my brother Frank pulls me out of my bed, I am on the floor. Quick, quick now my mother is pushing shoes on my feet, wrapping a blanket around us both and out the door! The devil is here. He has arrived in our village with the sun and brought his army. Frank has my hand, we run and run through the wood behind our house, branches slap into my face. We can hear dogs barking and the motor from the devil's bus. We lie in a ditch, cover ourselves with boards and leaves. My heart is loud.

Frank holds my hand, he covers my mouth with his other hand because I am crying. "Baby, baby, don't be a baby!" A spider grabs the end of my finger and bites into my arm.

Nyet! Nyet! I am dragged out by my foot, then picked up and carried by the waist. I bite the devil above his knee. "Jesus Christ!" he yells then ties me onto a seat in his bus. Mother, my mother, where is my mother? Other kids crying around me too. And yes. There she is, standing in front of the bus, her nightgown up and over her head. She is naked except for her boots and singing to me. The other mothers sing and strip too. The horn on the bus drowns out the singing, the driver of the bus laughs at her, my mother, then we are gone. I will not be allowed to live in my house again for six years.

But now, here we are, I am a man, riding in the back of the car with the bomb being built in my lap. I have a careful hand, careful touch and maybe it's a bump in the road but all of a sudden all is white and loud and I am pushing through, pushing through something strong but thin. It is my own head and here I am flying above the scattered car, my friends blood-spattered and still. I understand I am gone now, dead.

IRENE speaks as an adult.

I don't know how to imagine someone building a bomb. I just think of someone wrapping a present, all the careful tucks and folds, the sticky tape pulling at the hair on the back of your hand. Then an enormous red that is nearly impossible to tie, a slip knot that springs from the loop and explodes. Here. You hold this one. Poof. I press my hand against the sliding glass door. My hand is steady. I breathe and my breath is a grey oval on the glass, going, going, gone. But I am here, alive. Alive and kicking, acting, travelling, smoking up a storm. This past month I buried a friend. But this is not why I am afraid of the dark, no sir. I have buried him so deep he can't surface.

Where are the Doukhobors now? They are in split-level houses with satellite dishes, they are in the cities, impossible to spot in a crowd. The Sons of Freedom are nearly gone—some went to South America, a few are still in prison. Gilpin, the last Freedomite village, is just shacks now—poor, forlorn— like some of the reserves way up north.

But I keep looking for them, watching for a flash of eyes at night, peering out, looking for a distant fire between the trees. Black work. They used to say they were making a pillar of fire to join the earth to heaven. I need them now, a pack of rebels, lighting a fuse, making a protest, making a pillar of fire for all to see.

IRENE is fifteen, speaking to her truant officer again, one month later.

Miss Toye? Did you ever kidnap a Doukhobor kid? Because if you did this relationship is over, finito, done just one month after it's begun ... Well, good. And a very good morning to you too. Undoubtedly you are aware that during the month of September my attendance was flawless, I have become a model student, a beaten and sheep-like citizen of the world. In this time of great change and protest, I am silent. 1967 is a dark year in the life of me, Irene Dickson. But you are my refuge, Miss Toye. Between these four walls I feel free to speak my mind, my fears, my theories and beliefs—i.e., oftentimes when I am sitting there in class, trying to mind my own business, I am suddenly aware that I have large white antlers growing out of my head. They're all mossy and delicate. If I bump into anything you can bet it would hurt. I have to move through the halls carefully, getting anything out of my locker is murder. The sheer weight of these antlers, Miss Toye, my truant-officer-slash-game warden, makes me sleepy and, needless to say, totally incapable of fitting in.

You know if I was a true Doukhobor I'd hate your guts. I'd know all teachers, truant officers, counsellors, government etc. and so forth are corrupt through and through. I wouldn't trust you as far as I could spit but I do digress.

Wanna play teenager? Wanna play teenage Doukhobor? It is a game of my invention combining the basic elements of Doctor and Hide 'n' Seek. What if the one who's it takes off all her clothes, puts on a blindfold and everybody hides. Except everybody doesn't hide. Everybody sneaks back and makes a circle around you, a circle of gasoline. And when you yell "A hundred! Ready or not!" Whoosh! Up it goes, flames everywhere, and everyone's gone except your dog who's going nuts and half the world's gotta hear you screaming blue murder but nobody comes. Then finally this kid shows up, he watches you for a moment, calm as anything, then disappears and comes back with the garden hose and you're standing there bare-naked while he quietly smothers the fire that is raging around you. For months afterwards you wake up choking because you think your mattress has caught fire. You also think that brown thistles are growing in your throat.

Doukhobor means spirit-wrestler. There are three kinds. The Independent, the Community and the Sons of Freedom. The first two are highly normal and integrated and all. The Sons of Freedom are the ones you read about, highly persecuted—not unlike myself, my tribe. They keep only what is needed: i.e., eternal life and the golden rule. They avoid church, state, schools, regulations, authority, war. They cannot harm another living creature because the spirit of God is inside—watch me breathe.

I would like to live in a Doukhobor kitchen. They live very simply. I would like to be with them, living there again. Sitting on a hard wooden chair, drinking a glass of cold clear water. I think they are very fine human beings and that people who make fun of them are the ones who should be in jail. Perhaps people don't know how good the Doukhobors started out. Perhaps people don't know that Count Leo Tolstoy was their very good friend. And me too. Although I lived with them for only a short time, I, like Leo Tolstoy, am, and forever more shall be, a friend.

The boy who rescued me was Walter Dewitt. He had just moved into our neighbourhood. This was summer, 1963, the year of the great hunger strike. Paul Podmorrow said, "My heart is full of courage, brave to do something to make change, upheaval." He became my hero, Walter became my friend.

I thought Paul was beautiful, blue eyes and blond hair, a scarf at his neck but it was his determination, his sense of purpose and conviction that made him shine. I had a newspaper picture of him above my bed, and a chart, a calendar marking off the days. I never thought anyone would really die.

Walter, you know, he's a man of science. That's what he calls himself. He believes very much in the space age and in technology. He also knows the human body. And calm as anything he'd explain malnutrition and the process of starving. Then he'd get back to work: he's always making highly complicated plans to build a great city. He will design it, I will be in charge. All the buildings will be round, the cars will run on air and nobody will have to work anymore.

At night that summer we'd take the bus over the Lions Gate Bridge and wait for the nine o'clock gun. You know the nine o'clock gun, it's a cannon, or at least it was a cannon, now it's phony. I mean it goes off every night but it's just noise, a blank, an incredible sound that can be heard even here, bouncing around the mountains on the North Shore. Waiting for the nine o'clock gun is excruciating and a favourite pastime of various families and dogs and kids. Several stupid people, i.e., my brother and his friends, imitate the blast while they wait and these boys, they practise dying for all the hillside to see. But Walter and me are quiet, there is an understanding that if we are still enough maybe it won't happen. The rule is we aren't allowed to look at our watch or the gun itself.

But I can always tell when it's going to happen by looking at Walter. He gets this very weird look like he's seeing something, seeing something coming that no one else can see. I don't know how to tell if it's something great or something scary or just something boring. Walter? What is it? What do you see?

Bang! The ground rumbles underneath us. Our heads are alive with noise then splitting with the silence.

Look, Miss Toye, there in the distance, do you see them? Doukhobors, two of them, wearing black pants and suspenders. They're coming, they're coming. They're coming for me. They mean to save me, rid me, deliver me from the hands of strange children. They each hold a candle in one hand, a gallon of gas in the other. There is this roaring sound. It is the sound of everything being blown to smithereens. It is the sound of freedom.

> *IRENE ties her kerchief around her neck, and speaks in the voice of Paul Podmorrow, twenty-two years old, delirious.*

My prison is small. Bars at the door, bars at my bed. Don't come near me, doctor, teacher, devil. Don't talk to me, touch me, teach me words. I am a child of God, a child of my mother, my mother. Where is my mother? Paul! She is calling me in for supper, she is wrapping her big arms around me. But I am here, now, and this is a prison and I am a man. "We openly declare to all that we are on a hunger strike until death. The government refuses to investigate our matters and we protest." And now the devil is trying to stick a tube for feeding inside of me. I want to fight him but my arms are made of feathers and the fight is going out of me.

And then I am floating, above my bed and up, pushing through the walls, the ceiling, carried on the warm air of August above my prison and over the town of Hope. I have special sight. See the other Doukhobors, hundreds of them camped outside our prison, my brothers and sisters, singing psalms, making their breakfast, making a protest for all to see. They do not know yet what has happened to me—Paul Podmorrow, dead and gone now, child of God, child of the earth, Son of Freedom.

IRENE speaks as an adult.

This boy was a hero to me. When the strike started I would wake up in the middle of the night, knowing he was hungry. I had been dreaming him: when he opened his mouth thin blackbirds escaped. When he put his hand in mine it seemed drowned, yellow and puffed up. He never spoke but if he did it would be in a whisper. Sometimes he'd bring me gifts: a bright green bug cupped in his hands, a bowl of salt. What if his muscles came back strong as diamonds? What if he just stood up and walked straight through the bars and out the door? What if death's already in there, inside him? Come into his house like a goddamn rat.

The angels of God are good thoughts. Each living thing a church where he lives. Watch me breathe. Leaders. The Doukhobors were always looking for a leader, someone to take them home, away from here. They knew this place was just temporary, borrowed, their footprints barely formed before they would vanish. Poof. I am lost, lead me out. Take me by the hand, away from here.

>*IRENE at fifteen is talking to her truant officer, one month later.*

"Lighten up. These are the best days of your life." My friend Stan is always saying stuff like that to me, stuff designed to make me feel better that usually makes me feel like jumping off the nearest roof. Stan is the daytime security guard at the Marine Building which means he does zip. He is supposed to rid the building of kids like me but he doesn't. You know the Marine Building, right downtown, very old and sort of like the Empire State Building, like King Kong's going to be up top waving someone like you, Miss Toye, around in his fist. I consider its lobby to be my second home, my home away from home, my sanctuary. Stan is sixty-seven and used to be a farmer so he knows a thing or two about force-feeding. Stan believes no matter what that the government should've kept Paul Podmorrow alive. I don't know. I mean Stan is no intellectual but I do grant him his point of view.

Do you have a problem, Miss Toye? Exactly what is your problem? ... One day. I only missed one day of school. And I didn't *do* anything. I'm trying to come clean here. I just hitched over town and hung out with Stan at the Marine Building, end of story. When the strains of life and grade nine are too much for me, to the Marine Building I go. I am trying to explain to you, Miss Toye, some of the issues with which my mind grapples—life and death issues. Grapple, grapple.

And sometimes these issues keep me away from school and I don't like it any better than you. I was *not* running away again. I learned my lesson last year. I do not run away anymore. I face the trials of life head on. Even when I am deserted by all, I stand my ground. Antlered and weary, Irene Dickson, that is me.

Stan thinks I'm seventeen and that I'm a junior temp secretary for MacMillan Bloedel just up the street. I have no idea why I'm such a liar. I just am. I told the guy who gave me a ride home that I'm the youngest ever law student at U.B.C. I mean *the truth* is a very important issue to me but I mean in a general sort of way.

Okay, alright, I want to get this out. I also want you to swear yourself to secrecy, undying secrecy, Miss Toye. Agreed? I lied to you and everyone else about living with the Doukhobors. I didn't actually live with them. I just sort of visited last summer. Briefly. Very briefly. I went all the way up there, to the Kootenays, eight hours in a semi but the Doukhobors were not all that happy to see me. Or to be more precise they ordered me off their land which is a complete joke because they aren't supposed to own it in the first place.

But I just keep banging on the door, I am crying and making a fair amount of noise. Probably when they can't stand it any longer, they do let me in.

They are not proper Doukhobors. They are eating canned ham and watching "Car 54" on television. The world is full of phonies. These particular phonies have phoned the police to come get me.

I spend a terrible night in the home of the chief of police of Grand Forks. We're eating breakfast; the whole family is exhausted because I was awake the whole night and not exactly quiet about it. Despair is far too quiet a word for how I usually feel.

"Hey, you wanna see a real Doukhobor village?" The police chief is tapping me on the shoulder. And I say okay, that'd be alright, I'm pretty excited even. So off we go.

We drive for half an hour; very pretty country, snow-capped mountains etc., you expect to see Heidi and the whole gang around every corner. I am thinking of turning myself over to the Doukhobors, seeking asylum as they say. He parks the car in the middle of nowhere.

There is a gnarled old orchard and part of a barn. "Right up there," the chief points. A chimney, the black foundations of a house. "Used to be forty or more all crammed together under one roof, kids, husbands and wives, everyone married to one another and switching around ..." There is fireweed everywhere, other black marks on the ground that must have been woodsheds, stables ... The horseflies are glinting like fish and biting me. It's a stupid place and it's horrible, too quiet. It is the saddest and stupidest place on earth.

"Sometimes I live in the country
sometimes I live in the town
sometimes I get a great notion
to jump in the river and drown."

God I hate that song. Goodnight Irene, Irene goodnight, goodnight Irene. It is the most depressing song
ever written but most of the world is nuts about it
including my mother. How'd you like to be named
after the most depressing song ever written, except
even worse no one knows it's depressing, they sing
along like it was Rudolph the Red-Nosed Reindeer. No
one ever pays attention to anything. Undoubtedly
everything you are currently writing down is
unimportant.

"Irene goodnight, Irene goodnight
Goodnight Irene, Goodnight Irene
I'll see you in my dreams."

My parents come that afternoon to pick me up.
They're not angry, it's way worse than that. They're just
very disappointed. They have brought Walter with them
as a way of cheering me up.

He has this little booklet thing with him on the Hope
Slide which he must've bought on the way up. He reads
to me from it: "When Bill the trucker kissed his wife
goodbye that cold and dark January morning, he took
a bag lunch of corned beef on brown, his favourite,
and said, 'See you later.' Little did he know that tonnes
and tonnes of rock would cut short his journey and his
life."

Well, the real thing is even worse than the book. We
stop to look at it on the way home. The road just stops

and there's this huge pile of rocks and mashed up trees. You can't imagine it. It goes on for miles. But the worst part is the mountain that fell down, highly unnatural, like this big foot just kicked its face off.

Walter finds it all fascinating. "This is the end, this is the beginning of the end," I tell Walter. "Irene, give it a rest." Walter is sifting through the rocks and explaining—"There were two small earthquakes creating a crack in the surface. It is an act of nature. It doesn't *mean* anything."

"Mary Kalmakoff is buried here. She might be right under our feet." Walter is ignoring me. "Hers was the only body not found. Don't you find it rather interesting that ten miles on one side of Hope is the prison built specially for the Doukhobors, the place where Paul Podmorrow starved to death. And here, ten miles on the other side of Hope a mountain falls down and a Doukhobor girl is buried. Don't you find stuff like that incredibly weird?" "Not particularly," Walter tells me.

"Did you know the Doukhobors don't seek converts? They don't care who you are. They just want to be left alone. Walter! I'm talking to you. I'm trying to tell you they didn't want me, I wasn't allowed in, and I want in, somewhere ... I want to be right in the middle of something. I feel as though all great events in history happen just before I arrive."

"You could never be a Doukhobor anyway," Walter tells me. "Why?" Walter is carving his name into the rock, sometimes I really hate him. "Because, Irene. You're just too bossy." I promise then and there to never speak to Walter Dewitt again for the rest of my life. But on the other side of Hope, Walter starts talking to me:

"We will build a city. A great and wonderful city. A dome will protect us from the elements, from war, from all possible danger." And then Walter looks out the window and he sees that city. I can tell by his face that once again he is seeing what's invisible to me. What is it? What do you see?

IRENE lights four candles. She speaks as an adult.

Harry Kootnikoff killed by fire, Paul Podmorrow by hunger, Mary Kalmakoff swallowed by the earth, Walter Dewitt—a loss of hope.

When we were small, Walter always played at my house because Walter had one of those mothers who made you work when you visited. These mothers are famous within neighbourhoods, known and marked and avoided at all costs. When we were teenagers and went to his summer place to sneak beer and carry on, there was always a job that involved the septic tank, hoes and shovels. Septic tanks will always remind me of hangovers but I do digress.

So we'd be thirteen or so, and I'm supposed to go to Walter's house for the first time in ages because he has promised me his mother is out and we can't go to my house because I have ordered Walter off my property for a month, I can't remember why. I ring his doorbell and there's Walter, wearing cut-offs and his moon-shiner sweatshirt.

There are these marble balls, just inside the front door, when you come in. Two of them (*makes a head-sized circle with her hands*)—about so big. I don't know what they're supposed to be but Walter kicks off his runners and stands on one of these balls and starts rolling all over the wall-to-wall, up and down the halls. Incredible balance. "What do you think you're doing?"

He replies all calm and normal that he always uses these balls as a method of transportation within his own house. He was a real nutcase, Walter.

When Walter is dying I come running, come flying across the country and into his arms, arms held down by tubes and drugs and disease. For thirty years Walter has been my friend, my brother—sometimes I rescue Walter and sometimes Walter rescues me. I am part of a group of women—although we have boyfriends, husbands, lovers—the men we call in the middle of the night, the men we share the midnight scotch with, the friends of our childhood—they are often men who love other men and our men are dying.

Walter? He is almost gone, eighty-eight pounds, his skin puffed up and yellow. The name of his illness is unspeakable, ever since Walter was tested, he has refused to let us even mention the name of his disease. I am muzzled, frantic, and I hate it. Fight goddamn you, fight. I am a stupid girl who still believes that if I yell loud enough this won't happen. But it is happening all around us, the unimaginable, a mountain has fallen, hope is threatened, that nine o'clock gun was loaded all along. What if your muscles came back, strong as diamonds? What if I just picked you up and carried you out of here ...

Walter is leaving, pushing through. Decisions have been made, made bravely. For him hope is gone, but we are here and with you now, a little bit longer please.

I rub Walter's legs, feel the pulse drain out and he is gone.

Hope. It is a thing that is ever-changing but it's here, available. It is not soft. These days it has a dollar sign and a voice that is relentless, out on the street and howling. We are here, now, right in the middle of something. Fight. Hope ignites us into action. Makes a pillar of fire for all to see.

> *IRENE removes her shirt, fire suddenly comes up through a grate in the floor.*

I protest the deaths of these young men. My heart is full of courage, brave to make change, upheaval. I protest the deaths of these young men. My friends, my heart, my beautiful brothers.

> *The fire goes out. IRENE wraps herself up in a quilt.*

If I could sleep for twelve hours the world would be a better place. I am in a stranger's house, watching thin clouds cover the Kootenay moon, the stars, these are kind strangers, opening up their home to me. I will go back to my room. Tomorrow I will fly over the Hope Slide. It is getting more and more difficult to see the slide from the air, green covers the mountains, brave young trees planting themselves in impossible places, the lost highway now covered by shrubs and moss and all manner of living things. But I still remember the way it looked in the beginning, when the slide first happened, and that is something that can't be covered over. That memory is locked in and has affected now forever the way that I see. You can't really bury your friends, not ever.

Remember what I said about Walter and his incredible balance? This highly weird kid who could do something so special?

IRENE extends both arms, balances herself on invisible marble balls, looks ahead. She looks up. One arm reaches forward.

Walter? What is it? What do you see?

Little Sister

For my mother

Muriel Joan MacLeod (MacMillan)

Acknowledgements

This play was written with the generous support of the Ontario Arts Council and B.C. Cultural Services. *Little Sister* was a joint commission between Theatre Direct in Toronto and Green Thumb in Vancouver and I am indebted to Andrey Tarasiak and Patrick McDonald and the extraordinary support from both theatres. Thank you Big Strong Sisters—Joanna McIntyre for demanding so much, providing so much and making it work, and Kathryn Shaw for finding magic and intimacy in high school gymnasiums. I want to thank the cast, designers and composers in both cities, Cynthia Johnson from St. Paul's in Vancouver, and Katherine Gilday for the *The Famine Within*. Finally, thanks to the Banff Centre, not just for this play but for ten years—especially the behind-the-scene kindness of Carol Holmes and George Ross.

This script is, more or less, the one that premiered in the Theatre Direct production in Toronto. Because the Green Thumb production is a touring show, it is a slightly shorter, slightly revised version of this script.

Preface

When Joan MacLeod and I decided to work together, we began by talking about what was then current in each of our lives. We discovered that we both wanted to work with young people and that we had both been deeply affected by Katherine Gilday's documentary, *The Famine Within*, which is about how girls and young women feel about their bodies and how their shame robs them of their vitality and, in many instances, their lives. With the poetic simplicity that characterizes all of Joan's work, she moved into the complex realm of self-image and self-esteem and wrote *Little Sister.*

The three young women in the cast were all deeply affected by the experience and went through enormous changes themselves. It was my job to direct, but from the first day of rehearsal to the opening, Joan's instinct for the truth—coupled by her great good humour— inspired us all and kept us moving forward. Joan MacLeod's gift is her capacity for an unflinching empathy with those vulnerable recesses that most of us try to conceal. Though her commitment to her material is clear and strong, Joan's touch is always subtle. It was the unique combination of all of these skills and talents that made *Little Sister* such a transformative production.

—Joanna McIntyre

Little Sister was first performed in Toronto in February 1994—a Theatre Direct production at Canadian Stage's Berkeley Street (downstairs) with the following cast:

JAY . . . . .Andrew Dolha
TRACEY . . . . .Laurie Fraser
KATIE . . . . .Tamara Gorski
BELLA . . . . .Kim Kuhteubl
JORDAN . . . . .Sanjay Talwar

Directed by Joanna McIntyre
Set and Costume Design by David Rayfield
Lighting Design by Aisling Sampson
Stage Manager: L.J. Savage
Composer: Alan Cole
Flautist: Roxane Hreha
Dramaturge: Joanna McIntyre

Little Sister was then produced in Vancouver (Green Thumb touring show) March through June 1994 with the following cast:

JAY . . . . .Ian Butcher
TRACEY . . . . . .Daune Campbell
KATIE . . . . .Nicole LeVasseur
BELLA . . . . .Heather Troop
JORDAN . . . . .Nick Vrataric

Directed by Kathryn Shaw
Stage Manager: Michele Verhoeve
Set and Costume Designer: Helen Jarvis
Sound Designer: Greg Ruddell

The set is stark and simple. The only permanent, central part is the girl's washroom with it's essential elements being a full length mirror, a large trash can and a tampax machine. The other scenes happen around it. The row of lockers can be turned on its side for the Science table and for Katie's hospital bed. The running time is approximately eighty minutes. There is no intermission.

Scene 1

Girls' washroom. It is September, the first day of school. KATIE sits, an open notebook and pen in front of her. Slowly and meticulously she quarters and cores an apple, lines the sections up in front of her, and takes a bite. She picks up her pen and notebook, and she writes.

KATIE: Dear Dad: How-are-you-I-am-fine. Please say hello to Cynthia from me. Your apartment sounds nice. Hope there's enough room when I come at Christmas—ha, ha. Our new house is small and there are renters across the street.

Vancouver is awful, my new school is awful too—first day is almost over and I hate it. I miss Toronto, I miss private school.

Light remains on KATIE and also comes up on TRACEY and BELLA. BELLA drags TRACEY toward the washroom. TRACEY struggles unsuccessfully against her and yells loudly at the unseen JAY.

TRACEY: Hey! Jay! I'm talking to you!

KATIE: The kids here are all very …

TRACEY: *Hey asshole!*

KATIE: Tough.

BELLA: Tracey! C'mon!

TRACEY: Go make out with yourself in the mirror!

BELLA manages successfully now to pull TRACEY into the washroom. TRACEY struggles away from BELLA and yells out the door while KATIE carefully wraps up her sections of apple.

Why don't you go straight to hell!

TRACEY kicks the Tampax machine. KATIE closes her notebook protectively. TRACEY ignores KATIE and talks to BELLA.

Did you see what he was wearing? And he probably got up at six to do his hair.

BELLA: You two broke up, eh?

TRACEY: He's just so full of himself. "Jay! How're you doing?" I'm walking down the hall right? I haven't seen him for like *two* weeks and he just stares straight ahead. *Yo! Jay!* I'm thinking maybe he hasn't *heard* me, or maybe he's got *amnesia.* Maybe he *forgot* we went out every Saturday night the whole summer. (*to KATIE*) What are you staring at?

KATIE: Nothing.

BELLA: Tracey!

BELLA tries to introduce herself to KATIE but TRACEY cuts her off.

Hi. I'm ...

TRACEY carefully lifts a sweatshirt out of her pack.

TRACEY: This is his. He gave it to me. Correction. He left it on the beach when we were fooling around. I took it home and washed it in the sink; I washed it in Zero.

BELLA: Are you going to give it back?

TRACEY: I'm going to use it to hang myself. I'm going to hang myself from the condom machine in the guys' can. It'd serve him right. (*lighting a cigarette, to KATIE*) We're allowed to smoke in here.

BELLA: Liar.

KATIE: It's okay.

TRACEY: We should have a condom machine. That's sexual discrimination. Bella! What're you doing?

> *BELLA has taken a Thigh Master out of her pack. She places it between her legs, and pushes back and forth.*

BELLA: My goal is the Hallowe'en dance. Twenty-six pounds. That's my *first* goal. My *second* goal is Christmas. By then I will have lost forty which is too much but I want to lose ten more than I should so that I can eat what I want over the holidays. If I get a craving, like for chips, then I can use Thigh Master while I'm eating them. Thigh Master will destroy any damage done by the chips.

TRACEY: I thought it was called Thigh Buster.

BELLA: Thigh Buster's fake.

KATIE: Thigh Master is the original. It was invented by Suzanne Sommers.

BELLA: (*to KATIE*) I'm Bella. You're new, eh?

KATIE: (*nodding*) Katie.

BELLA: (*referring to TRACEY who cuts her off again*) This is …

TRACEY: I'm Madonna.

BELLA: Tracey! I'm going to the Hallowe'en dance as Madonna ... You know, Tracey, you could at least try to be nice. How'd you like to be the new person ...

TRACEY: How'd you like to try not being a queer.

BELLA: I'm not!

TRACEY: Only geeks get dressed up for Hallowe'en.

BELLA: You know how for grad they draw names for the people who don't have anyone to go with? Would you do that? Would you put your name in if you didn't have anyone to go with?

TRACEY: No. Christ, Bella, it's practically three years away.

BELLA: Even if it's the most important weekend of your life and you're going to miss it?

TRACEY: I don't intend to graduate. I intend to finish grade ten, work, get my own place then return to university when I'm thirty as a mature student.

BELLA: My mum says I'm too mature to wear a bikini. I'd put my name in. Grad's too big to miss.

TRACEY: Right. And go with Ga-Ga-Ga-Gordon or Sammy Pinto.

BELLA: What if you got Jay's name?

TRACEY: Like *he's* going to end up in the loser's bin. I don't think so.

BELLA: What if you got Jay's name and he didn't know it was you and when you showed up at the dance all dressed up he'd *completely* fall in love with you again.

TRACEY: I'd make him come to my house to pick me up. Jay'd be wearing some stupid rent-a-tux and when he opens our door I'm *doing it* with some guy on the kitchen floor. Or in a chair. Jay'd like that. He's a real pervert. I should give his name to Oprah Winfrey.

BELLA: Oprah's skinny again. She likes being skinny. She made a national statement.

KATIE: Oprah lost sixty-six pounds. She really took her time. This time it should work.

BELLA: When she got fat before she made a national statement that she liked being fat. Probably the skinny statement is what counts.

KATIE: For sure.

TRACEY: Jay should go on "Oprah" when she does her special pervert panel. And I'd be sitting there with the other victims and a team of expert pervert doctors. It'd serve him right.

KATIE returns to her notebook.

(*to KATIE*) Sorry your highness. We didn't mean to offend you.

KATIE: You didn't.

TRACEY: Where're you from?

KATIE: Toronto.

TRACEY: You have my sincerest sympathy.

BELLA: My aunt lives there. Rose Scarpacci. She's my mum's littlest sister. Unmarried. I guess you wouldn't know her.,

KATIE: No.

TRACEY: (*nudging BELLA*) C'mon. Let's go see if Jay's recovered.

BELLA: From what?

TRACEY: Amnesia. What do ya think?

BELLA: See you around Katie.

KATIE: See you around.

> *TRACEY and BELLA exit. KATIE unwraps and eats a piece of apple, then returns to her letter.*

Dad. This school is like something out of innermost New York City. Or Scarborough. You wouldn't believe it. Please tell me what date your holidays start at Christmas so I can get my ticket to visit. I don't want to go standby. I want to be sure. Love, love, love your loving daughter Katie.

Scene 2

JAY and JORDAN at JORDAN's locker

JORDAN: She does it on purpose. She's wearing this skirt the size of a *hanky* so that she can bend down and get stuff out of her locker, with this *ass*, this *perfect little ass* that she waves in the air. This happy face ass that says "Hi! Com'ere! Closer ..."

JAY: She's a bitch. Don't waste your time.

JORDAN: So I say, very polite: Hello Tracey, how was your summer? I tell her I'm going out for football and she thinks that's the funniest thing she's heard in her life.

JAY: She makes stuff up. All chicks do.

JORDAN: Then, *then* she tries to bum a smoke off me.

JAY: Did you give her one?

JORDAN: That isn't the point.

JAY: Oh man! And then I bet you gave her your homework. You see the new girl? She's incredible. Extremely classy. She's in my Science class ...

JORDAN: My problem is the alphabet. Tracey March, Jordan Martin ...

JAY: Everyone knows you do *all* Tracey's homework. You've got to see this new girl. I mean it.

JORDAN: Since kindergarten Tracey's always sat in front of me and since grade eight her locker's beside mine. In grade four she peed her pants. This big puddle under her desk. I didn't say anything. If I'd peed my pants she would've *broadcast* it—on the national news.

JAY: Every time I go to the beach this summer, she's there. As soon as she sees me she laughs like a maniac. I can't stand her laugh.

JORDAN: Ditto.

JAY: What I also can't stand is that she's been *waiting* for me. She's *pretending* she hasn't but it's so *obvious.*

JORDAN: I thought you were going out.

JAY: If there's no one else around, and I mean *no one,* we get together ...

JORDAN: Really.

JAY: The girl will do anything. She's highly perverted. Now we're back in school and she's pretending we had this big thing. I hate that kind of crap.

We hear TRACEY'S laugh offstage. JAY freezes. TRACEY and BELLA enter.

Shit. Here we go ... Ignore her.

TRACEY: Yo! Asshole!

JORDAN: What?

TRACEY: Not you Jordan ...

> *TRACEY carefully holds out a folded sweatshirt. She offers it to JAY.*

I believe this is yours.

JAY: Let's go buddy.

> *JAY snatches the shirt, examines it briefly, then lets it fall to the ground. A bell rings.*

Scene 3

KATIE sits at a table in the Science classroom. She writes to her dad.

KATIE: Dad. I just had History, the twentieth century. For my term project I have chosen World War II in its entirety. You wouldn't believe how slack the kids here are. They are incredibly ...

JAY enters, and takes his place beside KATIE.

Unfocused.

KATIE peers down a microscope.

JAY: American football has *four* downs. That means *four* chances to go ten yards. The CFL has three. So Canadian football is harder. It's not as much fun to watch. They're *crazy* for American football in England. It's the fastest-growing spectator sport on TV.

KATIE: (*referring to the microscope*) What do you see? You describe it and I'll write it down.

JAY looks down the microscope.

JAY: I see a big black thing, a big black thing with hundreds of little legs.

KATIE: Really?

JAY: Did you ever go to the dome in Toronto?

KATIE: Yes. Let me look.

KATIE looks down the microscope.

JAY: We should have our own team, major league. What d'ya see?

KATIE: I see the paramecium. I think it's the paramecium. It's swimming.

JAY: *What d'ya see at the dome?*

KATIE: *Aida.* I don't see any black thing with legs. I think you were seeing your own eyelash.

JAY: Who's Aida?

KATIE: It's an opera.

JAY: The Jays will choke this month. The World Series means shit.

KATIE: We only have ten minutes left. We aren't even halfway through the experiment and I don't want to …

JAY grabs the microscope.

JAY: I see *Mr. Paramecium* swimming over to *Mrs. Paramecium.* She's yawning. She's not in the mood.

KATIE: There is *no* Mr. and Mrs. That's the point. They reproduce by themselves. *That* is why we are supposed to cut the paramecium in half. *That* is why we should have cut the paramecium in half twenty minutes ago.

JAY: Poor guy.

KATIE: Then they'll be two. It doesn't die.

KATIE picks up a razor blade to slice the paramecium.

JAY: (*pause*) Would you rather be paralysed from the waist down or be retarded?

KATIE: Pardon me?

JAY: Terry Fox was incredible. I think they should have his statue on every corner. When he died I was in daycare. All the kids were bawling. We made a collage. Rick Hansen's incredible too. He's married. His wife is beautiful and they have a very *active* life if you know what I mean.

KATIE: *Please* look in the microscope. *Please* describe it so I can write down what you see. We're running out of time ...

JAY: I see a big black thing with ... No. Hold on. I see all these little white lines and ... I don't really see anything.

KATIE: We're going to fail. Our first experiment of the year and we're going to fail.

JAY: What's your problem? Are you in training to be a major scientist?

KATIE: I'm going to be a lawyer. My dad's a lawyer.

JAY: (*pause*) What if you got this guy, what if you had this case and you knew he was guilty? What would you do?

KATIE: I'm just going to finish this on my own. Okay?

JAY: What if he killed someone, what if he killed a kid? A whole whack of little kids. What if you were defending Clifford Olson?

KATIE: We're going to get in trouble for talking ...

JAY: The summer Clifford Olson was doing his thing we weren't allowed outside. We weren't allowed in our backyard even. We'd have to *drive* to the park and when we got there there'd be this *big pack* of paranoid mothers. It was awful.

KATIE: You broke the slide.

JAY: What?

KATIE: You must've hit it with the lens. You wrecked the slide.

The bell rings.

This is great. This is just great.

JAY: Just write it up like we did it. We've got tonight to write it up.

KATIE: I've got a math test tomorrow.

JAY: We saw the paramecium, we described the paramecium

KATIE: You killed the paramecium.

JAY: We cut him in half. What do you know! Presto! Two parameciums.

JAY exits. KATIE opens her notebook to write to her dad.

KATIE: Dad. With regard to the contract we made concerning my marks—that is you sending me to computer camp if I keep up my average. I am a little concerned about Science because we are graded as a team. My partner is a real Neanderthal type, quite likely learning disabled. Please let me know when I'm supposed to come at Christmas. You can just put the date on a piece of paper with the support cheque. You don't have to write a letter. Love, love Katie.

Scene 4

BELLA and TRACEY are in the washroom. BELLA is eating, TRACEY is checking herself out in the mirror, applying make-up throughout.

BELLA: I blew my diet. This is last weekend, my cousin Christina's wedding. I *love* weddings. Christina looked *great*. She wanted to lose fifteen pounds for her dress and she did. The food was *incredible*—mountains of it but *nothing, absolutely nothing* that I'm allowed to eat. I spend *twenty* minutes hunting for something, celery, a carrot stick. Nothing.

I ate some gnocchi, just a taste. Then medallions of veal in a cream sauce and some clams with linguini. I ate four pieces of garlic bread in about three seconds. I will not even tell you about the desserts because you'd be absolutely disgusted.

TRACEY: (*lighting a cigarette*) Paula Abdul's fat. I saw her last night on "Much". Katie thinks so too ...

BELLA: Fat! God! What do you two think when you look at me?

TRACEY: We think you're big-boned.

A bell rings.

C'mon.

The girls begin to walk to their History class.

BELLA: I lost eight pounds last week and now I've gained it all back in two days.

TRACEY: Give it a rest, Bella. You always look the same to me.

> *A slide of a concentration-camp victim from World War II is projected on a screen. TRACEY stops a moment and yells at an unseen admirer. She cocks her hip out. A silhouette of her body momentarily covers the screen.*

Hey you! Yeah! What are you staring at? Why don't you take a picture!

Scene 5

*BELLA and TRACEY sit with JORDAN and JAY,
looking up at the slide. JAY changes his place to get
away from TRACEY. KATIE takes her place, standing
in front of the slide. She reads nervously from a stack
of papers.*

KATIE: And during the great famine that began in
May 1940 during the German occupation of the
Netherlands, the Dutch authorities maintained
rations between six hundred and a thousand
calories a day.

BELLA noisily unwraps a package of licorice.

This is characterized as semi-starvation. When
they had lost twenty-five percent of their body
weight, the Dutch were given crisis food-
supplementation.

In the Lodz Ghetto in 1941 besieged Jews were
allotted starvation rations of five to twelve hundred
calories a day.

*The slide goes black, lights dim to half. BELLA eats her
licorice. JORDAN exits. TRACEY exits sexily, trying to
get JAY's attention. JAY watches KATIE gathering her
papers, then he follows her out.*

JAY: That was excellent.

KATIE: Pardon me?

JAY: Your project. And highly interesting. You want some lunch or something?

KATIE: No thank you.

JAY: I've got my dad's car and ...

KATIE: I don't eat lunch.

JAY: That's cool. Well.

> *KATIE walks off. JAY yells out after her.*

I really did enjoy watching ... (*to himself*) you.

Scene 6

TRACEY is at her locker, rolling up her skirt a notch. JORDAN enters.

TRACEY: What are you staring at?

JORDAN: Good morning, Tracey.

TRACEY: I should report you for sexual harassment. I could, you know. Remember that creepy old professor who stared at the girls in swimming? He's in jail now. Up the creek.

JORDAN: He is not in jail.

TRACEY: Death row. That's where you're going to end up. Look. I want you to imagine there's this invisible wire that separates your locker from mine and if you touch it you're going to explode, die on contact.

JORDAN: I thought the rule was I'm supposed to turn my back and stare in the opposite direction when you're at your locker.

TRACEY: Correct. That is the rule. Do you have any smokes?

JORDAN: Yes. Yes I do, Tracey. Why don't you take the whole pack?

TRACEY: Really?

JORDAN: And here's my English essay. I was up all night working on it but why don't you just rub out my name and hand it in for yourself?

TRACEY: That's like a joke, right? You have a real dazzling sense of humour, Jordan. You're one witty guy.

JORDAN: Did you hear about Jay?

TRACEY: What?

JORDAN: I can't remember.

TRACEY: What? What! Jordan! God you're an asshole.

JORDAN: Katie passed out in Science. He picked her up and carried her to the nurse's office. A regular knight in shining armour.

TRACEY: Is this supposed to be a big deal? Like he's up for some medal for bravery? It's not as if he went into a burning building. That really makes me sick.

JORDAN: What?

TRACEY: You make me sick.

JORDAN: Has anyone ever told you, Tracey, that your conversations lack a certain focus. You jump from one subject to another then ...

TRACEY: So I bet you're really pissed off about football, eh? I bet you're pissed off you didn't make the team ...

JORDAN: The subject we were discussing was Jay. Jay and Katie.

TRACEY: Maybe you could go out for synchronized swimming. Or curling. You'd be one hell of a curler, Jordan.

JORDAN: I like Katie. She's pretty. And very smart.

TRACEY: You could wear those dorky pants and curling shoes with little tassels. And one of those team jackets with this little thingee on the sleeve except instead of saying Jordan it says *asshole.* And for your information, *dork,* Katie is *not necessarily smart.* Just because someone is *quiet* and *weird* it doesn't mean they're smart.

JORDAN: Yeah but you're loud and you're ...

TRACEY: What?

JORDAN: Failing math.

TRACEY: Right there on your sleeve—first rate, utter wimp, absolute asshole!

TRACEY slams her locker door and storms off. Half light on JORDAN, catching himself in a hidden mirror inside his locker. He takes out a comb and works hard at his hair.

Scene 7

Girls' washroom. BELLA and KATIE are poring over a fashion magazine. On the screen we see the images of the super models that the girls are seeing. Each comment signifies a new slide.

BELLA: If I was allowed to wear short skirts I'd wear this in a second.

KATIE: Your mum won't let you?

BELLA: I won't let me.

KATIE: You could wear tights, black tights ...

BELLA: I'd be killed on sight ... Now that's pretty.

KATIE: But she isn't ... It looks nicer when their hips are small ...

BELLA: Like yours ...

KATIE: Oh please! I've always been big down there ... She's beautiful.

BELLA: She looks like a corpse.

KATIE: I don't think so!

BELLA: Like her whole body got run over by a steamroller, like in the cartoons.

They turn a page.

BELLA & KATIE: (*in unison*) Ugly!
KATIE: She *can't* be a model.

BELLA: What is she?

KATIE: A lawyer, human rights. My dad's girlfriend is a lawyer but she's beautiful. Like Farrah Fawcett only younger ... Ugh! Look at this one. Yuck.

Enter TRACEY.

BELLA: (*reading*) "This financial planner and mother of three still makes time to volunteer in her community" ... Maybe they're make-overs. Maybe these are the before pictures.

TRACEY: Maybe they're dykes, like you two.

KATIE: Ha, ha.

TRACEY: So. How's Jay?

KATIE: How should I know ...

BELLA: Do you think the fat girl in Wilson Phillips is secretly depressed? Do you think it drives her nuts that she doesn't look like the other two?

TRACEY: Jesus, Bella. Give it a rest. You're obsessed.

BELLA: Just because you don't have to worry about what you eat ...

TRACEY: You're right Bella. I wake up every morning and the very first thing I do is thank God that I have a perfect life ... Sorry. I'm on the rag.

BELLA: Me too. It makes my weight go up.

TRACEY: Bella!

BELLA: Well, it does. I'm okay. I'm back on my diet.

KATIE: (*by rote*) You should eat grapefruit. They create a chemical reaction that aids digestion. You should eat half a grapefruit before every meal. Or a glass of grapefruit juice but check to see first that it has no sugar in it. Natural fruit juices only. It's probably safer to just eat the real grapefruit. A medium-size one is only ninety calories.

TRACEY: I hear you passed out in Science and Jay pulled the big He-Man number.

KATIE: I fainted. Sometimes I faint at the sight of blood.

TRACEY: Dissecting a trout? They don't even have proper blood. They have weird fish blood.

BELLA: What did you get on your History project?

TRACEY: *C* minus.

BELLA: I got a *B*. Katie?

KATIE: *A*.

TRACEY: I brought in my grandpa's medals from World War II. I should have got higher.

BELLA: But you didn't write a report.

TRACEY: I labelled them!

BELLA: What does it feel like to faint?

KATIE: Like pins and needles then everything black. I used to pass out in church when I was little.

BELLA: My mum threw a fit this weekend because I missed mass. I was up until four on Saturday night because I'm on the decorating committee for the dance. I slept in. She thinks I'm going to hell.

TRACEY: I don't have to talk to my mum. We have an arrangement. From four until six I don't have to talk to anyone in my house. This is *supposed* to make up for me not having my own place. Whoopee …

BELLA: (*to KATIE*) Your mum's pretty.

KATIE: No she's not!

BELLA: I saw her dropping you at school. I think she's pretty.

TRACEY: Are your mum and dad divorced?

KATIE: Separated. I'm going to live with my dad next year. They want me to live with them.

Getting up hurriedly to exit, KATIE drops her notebook. TRACEY notices; KATIE does not.

TRACEY: What's Jay going to do? Is he going to write you letters?

KATIE: No!

TRACEY grinds out her cigarette. She yells after KATIE who is now fleeing from the washroom.

TRACEY: All I'm saying is you should be careful! That's Jay's idea of heaven—a passed out chick.

Half lights on TRACEY picking up the notebook. KATIE slumps down against the lockers. JAY looks toward KATIE but is in a different reality.

Scene 8

JAY slowly approaches KATIE throughout.

JAY: I pick her up. I have excellent upper-arm strength; I bend carefully, from the knees. I pick her up. I can press 220. She is light as anything, an empty box. I pick her up. She feels good against me, warm and tiny.

JAY picks up KATIE. She is curled up against him, unconscious.

Katie. Did I tell you? Last year at the PNE parade I held my little sister, held her up in my arms for two hours so that she could see. My neck, my shoulders, everything is so sore and aching but I kept holding her up and above all the others. So if you ever feel like you are going to faint again, I mean it, you can just fall right here, onto me. No problem little sister. Lean on me.

JAY continues to hold KATIE. Lights up on TRACEY who reads from the notebook KATIE has left in the washroom.

TRACEY: Dear Dad: How-are-you-I-am-fine. I am very disappointed about Christmas too but I do hope you have a relaxing time in Costa Rica. We will be going to grandma's in Victoria. Wishing you and Cynthia a very happy holiday season. Katie.

TRACEY's light goes out. JAY tenderly puts KATIE down; she is very shaky. A mirror hall spins light all around. It is Hallowe'en night now, and KATIE slow-dances with JAY in the half light that remains.

Scene 9

JORDAN, BELLA and TRACEY are in the washroom,
passing around a bottle of beer. BELLA is dressed like
Madonna.

JORDAN: Did you want to dance, Madonna?

BELLA: It's okay.

TRACEY: Don't even ask. I have a boyfriend you know.

BELLA: Since when do you have a boyfriend?

TRACEY: Since last weekend. But it feels a lot longer
for both of us. His name is Jean-Claude. He's very
French and a hundred times more sensitive than
these bozos we have around here. He's nineteen
but we don't notice the age difference at all.

BELLA: Does he go to U.B.C.?

TRACEY: He's a tree planter. But he's currently
collecting UIC.

JORDAN: So where's Jean-Claude tonight, Fifi?

TRACEY: He doesn't come to little-kid dances.

JORDAN: Et tu? Pourquoi est-tu ici seule …

TRACEY: What?

JORDAN: Don't you and and Jean-Claude parlez-vous
francais …

TRACEY: We communicate in other ways. But that's something you wouldn't know about, Jordan ...

Half lights on JORDAN, TRACEY and BELLA. Lights up on JAY and KATIE dancing. JAY is all over KATIE. KATIE dances woodenly. JAY kisses KATIE lightly; she doesn't respond.

JAY: Your lips are dry.

KATIE: I'm sorry.

JAY: I like them. I like all of you.

JAY tries to kiss KATIE again.

KATIE: Don't ...

JAY: Do you know the first time I saw you? It wasn't Science. It was the morning before. You were standing on the steps outside the gym and I was at practice. It looked like the light was shining right through you. You're so beautiful Katie.

KATIE: Tracey'll get mad.

JAY: Look, whatever she told you, it's ... it's nothing. I'm at this party last weekend and she's crying and all that crap. I'm almost feeling sorry for her. Then she starts making out with this little weasly guy. Right in front of a million people. You're so different. You're so perfect.

KATIE: Don't say that.

JAY: Every little part of you.

KATIE backs away from JAY. She leaves him standing there in the scattered light. Lights come up on the others in the washroom.

TRACEY: I wish my brother would die. Well, not actually die but maybe go into a big coma and not wake up until I had my own place. And when he did wake up he'd have like a totally different personality.

BELLA: I love my brothers.

TRACEY: Jordan probably loves your brothers too.

JORDAN: Bella, let's dance. Right now. I mean it.

BELLA: I can't.

JORDAN: Why?

BELLA: I ripped my costume. It's sort of tight.

KATIE enters. She is very shaky.

TRACEY: We're allowed to drink in here.

KATIE: Ha, ha.

TRACEY: How's your boyfriend?

KATIE: I don't have a boyfriend, I don't want a boyfriend, ever.

TRACEY hands KATIE a beer. The four of them pass it around.

Is it light?

TRACEY: Light as air.

KATIE: Jordan, what are you doing in here?

TRACEY: It's not a guy. It's Jordan.

JORDAN: Okay. That's it. I mean it. You know what you are, Tracey?

TRACEY: I-know-you-are-so-what-am-I?

JORDAN: You are a first-rate little bitch. You also owe an apology to Bella.

BELLA: Why?

JORDAN: (*to BELLA*) She made fun of you. She imitated you behind your back when you were dancing with Sammy.

BELLA: Tracey ...

KATIE slumps over against JORDAN.

JORDAN: Katie? You okay? Katie ...

TRACEY: Oh great. She passes out on like two sips of beer.

JORDAN: She didn't have any beer.

BELLA: Yes she did.

JORDAN: She didn't swallow. She's like me ... I don't inhale smoke either.

KATIE begins to come to. Her speech is unclear.

TRACEY: Give her some water, Bella. Give her some of your juice.

KATIE: (*bats the juice box away*) Get that away from me.

JORDAN: We should get Mrs. Simms.

KATIE: No ...

TRACEY: You're not getting the nurse, Jordan. We'll get in shit for drinking.

JORDAN: She's sick.

KATIE: Don't tell my parents. Don't tell my dad ...

TRACEY: He's in Toronto. How're we going to tell?

KATIE begins to shake uncontrollably.

She's nuts. Jay probably got her loaded ...

KATIE faints.

BELLA: Katie!

JORDAN: Tracey! Put your jacket under her head, *now!* Bella, turn her on her side if she starts choking. Tracey! Move!

TRACEY: I'm not touching her. You're not supposed to mess with a messed-up person.

JORDAN and BELLA tend to KATIE. They carry her to a table in the Science room and cover it with a sheet. The table is now a hospital bed with IV attached. TRACEY hasn't moved. She lights a cigarette and yells to the others.

You could hurt her even worse by helping!

She notices JAY still caught in the light. She yells at him.

Hey! Jay! Yeah asshole! I'm talking to you!

JAY doesn't respond.

Jay! Listen! Did you hear what happened? Your girlfriend's out cold! Totally wasted. No lie. So ... So. Did you want to do something? You and me?

Light comes up on KATIE, alone, sitting weakly on the side of the bed. She covers her mouth in panic, as if remembering she just did something terrible. Although TRACEY and KATIE are unaware of each other, it is as if TRACEY now speaks for KATIE.

I am talking here! ... C'mon! ... Somebody! Listen! (*defeated, to herself*) I'm trying ... I am trying to talk to you.

   Blackout.

Scene 10

Spot up on KATIE wearing a hospital gown. She is sitting on the edge of the bed. She is exhausted. She struggles to keep her head up. Half light on JAY watching her. JAY is in a different reality from KATIE.

KATIE: Dear Dad: My stomach is a clear clean space. My blood is water and my bones are made of balsa wood. My skull is china and my skin, a thin wash of paint. I am hollow as a negative and when I leave there will be no trace, no trace of me. With love your loving daughter Katie.

Lights up on JAY. He walks toward KATIE tentatively.

JAY: I go to see her. I bring flowers. I bring her *Vogue* and *Seventeen Magazine.* She doesn't want to see me, Katie won't see me. The head nurse puts the flowers in a vase—Children's Hospital written on the side. She holds the magazines out in front of her as if they stink, as if I've brought in pornography.

JAY stops abruptly as if he's encountered a wall of glass. KATIE continues; she is suddenly very angry.

KATIE: P.S. I wish to report a breach of contract. The contract, between myself and this hospital was as follows: If I ate my yogurt I could study tonight and miss group. The contract was *not* for yogurt with fruit on the bottom and thus the said contract should be rendered null and void ...

JAY looks directly at KATIE. She does not see him; she stares at the floor throughout.

JAY: Katie! Yo! C'mon ... You don't even have to open your mouth. Just look up. Just look at me.

Lights fade on JAY. He exits. Half light remains on KATIE. Very slowly and with exhausted difficulty throughout the next scene as BELLA and TRACEY talk, KATIE will remove the gown. Her sweat pants and T-shirt are underneath.

Scene 11

BELLA and TRACEY in the washroom, a few days later.

TRACEY: Anorexic.

BELLA: No way.

TRACEY: Absolutely. Anorexic. As in Karen Carpenter.

BELLA: Who?

TRACEY: As in Shannen What's-her-name and half of Hollywood for God's sake.

BELLA: Katie's anorexic? Katie thinks she's fat? That's impossible …

TRACEY: She's nuts. Part of the disease is being totally mental.

BELLA: I wish I had that. I wish I was anorexic just for a week. I mean I wish I was skinny like that but cured. You know what I mean.

TRACEY: She's at Children's. The fruitcake ward. Correction. The ultra-lite-slim-fast-fruitcake ward.

BELLA: We should go see her. I've never even been in a hospital overnight, except when I was born. I didn't really mean that … about wishing I had it. Anorexia. I wonder how she got it?

TRACEY: Maybe Jay gave it to her …

BELLA: Oprah had these ladies on, the kind that eat a ton of ice cream and then throw it all up.

TRACEY: Bulimics.

BELLA: I mean they're all totally cured now but this one lady she got to the point that she threw up so much she couldn't do it anymore so she got her husband to kind of grab her from behind and help her.

TRACEY: Maybe Jay told Katie he likes his women skinny. He does that. He tries to make people insecure.

BELLA: And even the cured ladies on "Oprah", all of them, even though they're happy now, every single one said that every time they look in a mirror they can't see themselves. They can't really see what they look like. They just see all the flaws, all the parts of them they don't like ... I do that.

TRACEY: Everybody does that. Not liking the way you look is completely normal. The whole world could go on "Oprah" and complain about something. The only people who are thrilled with their appearance at all times are guys. Jay practically has an orgasm every time he walks by a mirror.

BELLA: Tracey ... Did you and Jay have sex?

TRACEY: Sort of.

BELLA: How do you sort of have sex?

TRACEY: We didn't have real sex. We just fooled around quite a bit. Correction. He fooled around. He made sure he got what he wanted and then called it a night.

BELLA: But it was safe ...

TRACEY: I invented safe sex. Of course it was safe.

BELLA: And you don't think you're too young for sex and all?

TRACEY: If this was the Middle Ages we'd both be grandmothers.

BELLA: When did they invent mirrors?

TRACEY: I don't know. Probably lady dinosaurs looked at their reflections in the lake and threw a fit about the size of their heads. How should I know?

BELLA: They had tiny heads, the dinosaurs. That's why they didn't survive.

TRACEY: If they were survivors they could've gone on "Oprah". Oprah's crazy for survivors.

BELLA: Poor Katie. I hope she'll be okay.

TRACEY: Let's see.

Scene 12

JAY and JORDAN are at JORDAN's locker.

JAY: She won't see me. I've tried twice now.

JORDAN: Katie's sick. She probably doesn't want to see anybody.

JAY: I keep thinking I came on too strong. She's real fragile, right? I probably scared her to death. But I was always telling her she's pretty. And how can she possibly think she's fat. She's perfect.

JORDAN: I don't think it's that simple.

JAY: That's how it works. Some girls have it for years. I mean it.

JORDAN: Katie's smart. She'll get over it.

JAY: This isn't the first time she's been in the hospital for this shit ... Don't tell anyone.

JORDAN: Bella already got this card for everyone to sign. Her and Tracey are going to see her.

JAY: Tracey! Shit ... You just said she doesn't want to see anyone. Or maybe it's me. Maybe she just doesn't want to see me. Why don't you go, go talk to her, Jordan. All girls like you.

JORDAN: All girls like me? Since when?

JAY: I mean you're, you know, like a friend to all women.

JORDAN: Where are all these girls that like me?

JAY: Just tell her I care and all that stuff. You know what to say.

JORDAN: Yeah. I always know what to say.

JAY: Chicks are nuts about guys who talk. That's like a gift. You should use it more to your advantage.

JORDAN: Can I ask you something?

JAY: Shoot.

JORDAN: Why Katie? What is she to you? The ultimate challenge …

JAY: No!

JORDAN: Going where no man has dared to go before …

JAY: Piss off …

JORDAN: She's really sick you know. Girls die from this all the time.

JAY: You think I don't know that? I just want … I want to help.

JORDAN: That's good, I guess …

> *JAY begins to exit. JORDAN carefully takes a battered notebook from his locker, looks at it for a moment, then puts it in his backpack. JORDAN walks toward the hospital area. JAY returns to the lockers. He yells out after JORDAN who is already out of range.*

JAY: I just want to look after her!

> *JAY paces then slumps against JORDAN's locker. He looks toward the others.*

Scene 13

JORDAN, BELLA and TRACEY are gathered around KATIE's bed KATIE is distracted and not at all pleased to see them.

BELLA: Tracey used to eat dirt when we were little. I mean really eat it. Big handfuls of the stuff.

TRACEY: And you ate paste.

BELLA: Everyone ate paste. I saw a guy on TV who was eating a truck, an eighteen-wheeler, it took him years … You know what this is like? Like that joke-thing: don't think of hippopotamuses and all day its stuck in your mind, it's all you want to say. Hippopotamus! Hippopotamus! I keep thinking we shouldn't talk about, you know, food and eating and …

JORDAN: Bella, you're motoring …

BELLA: Hospitals make me nervous.

KATIE: It's okay … I really should get some sleep. Thanks for coming. Thanks for the card.

TRACEY: We just got here … You look good. You look okay.

KATIE: Fat.

BELLA: Katie, you look beautiful.

KATIE: I have been gaining one pound a day for eleven, excuse me, eleven and a half days. *Don't* tell me I look good.

JORDAN hands KATIE a stack of papers.

JORDAN: These are my notes from English and History. I know you have a tutor and all but I just thought it might help if you had notes from another student too.

KATIE: Thanks.

BELLA: Everybody misses you ...

JORDAN hands KATIE his notebook.

JORDAN: And this is a journal I kept in grade eight. I was in a hospital too. My mum died and I sort of went nuts. I'm supposed to call it a breakthrough. Not a breakdown. People get sad, Katie.

KATIE: I know that. Thanks.

BELLA: In fact probably a lot more kids than you realize get very depressed and feeling worthless and all.

KATIE: Believe me. *I do not* think I'm worthless.

TRACEY: How come there's a little kid in here? How come there's a kid in the room next to you?

KATIE: She's here for the same reason as me.

TRACEY: You mean she won't eat? Doesn't she like candy? All kids like candy.

BELLA: Hippopotamus! Hippopotamus! I've got a whole bunch of them in there now, just lodged inside my brain.

KATIE: Somehow that seems a rather fitting image to have *stuffed* inside your head, Bella. Ha, ha.

BELLA: When are you going home?

KATIE: Friday. My internist says maybe before, if I can reach my target weight.

TRACEY: What's that?

KATIE: *That* is none of your business.

BELLA: Are you going to Toronto for Christmas?

KATIE: Look. I am really tired ...

TRACEY: Or Costa Rica? Visit your dad?

KATIE: What? How did you know ...

TRACEY: I'm going to my dad's in Prince George for Christmas ...

KATIE: My father is *not* going to Costa Rica ...

TRACEY: You ever been to Prince George? It stinks. Literally. But it's pretty. We're going cross-country skiing. Last year we went ice-fishing on Christmas Eve. My dad's great. He never gives me shit. He finds me highly amusing and we're really looking forward to Christmas together.

KATIE: If he's so great and you're so great then why don't you live with him?

TRACEY: I live with my mum. You know something? You were a lot nicer before you got sick.

KATIE: Nice girls don't eat ...

JORDAN: You take care, Katie. We'll see you after Christmas.

TRACEY: And for your information, Katie, just because you don't live with someone it doesn't mean they don't love you. Any dork knows that.

BELLA: Bye, Katie.

JORDAN and BELLA exit. JAY kicks TRACEY's locker violently then exits.

KATIE: Sorry. Nice girls always apologize first. I'm sorry. There. Now you must be happy, please leave.

TRACEY: You don't have to say anything to me ...

KATIE: Actually, nice girls are never in the position of having to apologize. Nice girls do everything perfectly.

TRACEY: I don't think you're perfect. In fact you're a really lousy visit. I hope you get home soon, Katie.

KATIE: Bye.

TRACEY puts a cigarette in her mouth and exits. KATIE gets out of her bed as if to run after the others then changes her mind. She crawls back into bed. She is very upset.

Nice girls get up in the morning, exhausted of course, but they still like the morning best. They always jog an hour before breakfast then drink one half a glass of grapefruit juice—one half, on Fridays they drink one quarter.

KATIE is trying very hard to gain back some control. She reaches for her notebook; she tries to talk sweetly.

Dear Dad. I am feeling much, much better. I am sorry you cancelled your trip to Costa Rica. Don't

worry about me! Everyone here says I'm doing fine.
They are all very proud of me.

*KATIE tears up the paper. She is furious, out of bed,
pacing.*

I make lunch, make lunch for me and Buddy and
Andrew. Mummy's little helper. I put six slices of
bread on the counter, *six*. The bread is soft and big
and brown. I cover the bread with peanut butter
because I *love love love* peanut butter. I slice up
bananas and put them on top. Then four hey-dey
cookies apiece into little plastic bags *and* one big
red apple for me.

I *don't* jog to school. I get a ride with mum but I
make her let me out a block before so no one will
see I'm with her. I study right until the bell.

I always eat lunch in the girls' washroom, always
sit under the Tampax machine. I've never had a
period and think by sitting under the machine this
will somehow help. I realize this is not very logical
but to the best of my knowledge I am the only girl
in grade ten who hasn't started. I take the sandwich
apart. I scrape all the peanut butter off the little
slices of banana and eat them slowly. I eat the
crusts, I *love* crusts. I don't even look at the cookies,
I keep them hidden inside the bag and then I
throw the bag into the trash. Let's do lunch.

The last class of the day is History. On my way to
class I feel clear as spring water, clear as glass, when
I move through the halls, I am moving in a glass
box. I take my seat. When I leave there will be no

impressions, no trace of me. I put my hands around my waist because my stomach is crying.

Slides of the Holocaust. There is no way of knowing who lived or died. Who are the survivors? I am feeling badly for the victims of Auschwitz as is the rest of my class but I am more concerned about the four hey-dey cookies in my brown recycled lunch bag in the trash.

I want to dive through to the bottom, dive into the thrown-out sandwiches, butts, damp paper towels, apple cores and surface with *my lunch,* a giant pearl I can stuff inside and swallow and swallow …

Don't. I am afraid of the sound of my stomach, afraid my bones make noise inside my skin when I walk up the aisle but I am *most* afraid because the inside of my mouth tastes like peanut butter and *it should not.*

KATIE breaks down. She curls up on her bed.

Somebody! … Listen! Help me please!

KATIE rings the bell above her bed.

I'm hungry! I am so hungry …

Blackout.

Scene 14

BELLA and TRACEY are in the washroom on a January morning, one month later.

BELLA: We had fifty-three people for Christmas dinner. We had to borrow chairs and tables from the church. The little kids ate in the rec room but it was still packed. My mum cooked for two weeks non-stop. I'm not exaggerating.

TRACEY: Do Italians eat turkey?

BELLA: We do. Plus everything else under the sun.

KATIE enters.

You made it home for Christmas, eh?

KATIE: Christmas Eve. My dad flew in on the 23rd. It was great. Cynthia didn't come. How was Prince George?

TRACEY: We went to the Keg.

BELLA: For Christmas dinner?

TRACEY: Puh-leeze! New Year's. It was excellent.

KATIE: My dad bought me a mountain bike and a skirt from Laura Ashley. On Boxing Day we went to Whistler and rented this place. The whole family. Even my mum was great. It was just like how it used to be. What'd you get?

BELLA: Four dresses, homemade, all ugly. And a membership at the 'Y.' Tracey? What'd you get?

TRACEY: A bus pass.

KATIE: That's a neat present.

TRACEY: I asked for a car. In seventy-three days I'm going to get my learner's. Ask me a question. Any question. I've already memorized the whole book. C'mon, Bella.

BELLA: I don't know ...

TRACEY: Any question.

KATIE: Required distance from a fire hydrant for parking?

TRACEY: Five metres. Ask something hard. When I get my real license this is what I'm going to do. First thing, I'm going to drive to Seattle. A car is like having your own place but better because you're mobile. Guys have known this stuff for years. It's going to be great.

BELLA: Can I come?

TRACEY: Possibly.

KATIE: You know something, Tracey? Thinking one event or one person is going to change your life ... it's dangerous. It'll still be you behind the wheel. A car isn't going to make all your problems go away.

TRACEY: What problems? Do I look like someone with problems?

KATIE: Actually yes.

TRACEY: Pardon me?

KATIE: Change doesn't happen overnight ...

TRACEY: When did you get so mouthy?

KATIE: Nice girls don't speak?

TRACEY: Look Katie, we're all real glad that you're recovered and all but that doesn't give you the right to ...

KATIE: I'm just saying that thinking one person or one thing is going to solve all your problems ...

TRACEY: I know what this is.

KATIE: What?

TRACEY makes the sign of the cross, protecting herself from KATIE.

BELLA: What are you doing?

TRACEY: Therapy. Am I right? You're in therapy.

KATIE: I go to a group ...

TRACEY: I knew it. You're talking like my mum; my mum did therapy.

BELLA: That's great, Katie. Good for you.

TRACEY: Therapy in ten words or less—

TRACEY counts off each word on her fingers.

I-love-you, you're-an-ass-hole, let's-hug, exclamation-mark.

Scene 15

In the hall, JAY runs deliberately right into TRACEY.

TRACEY: Watch where you're going.

JAY: I want to talk to you.

TRACEY: I'm busy.

TRACEY tries to continue walking. JAY grabs her.

Keep your goddamn hands offa me.

JAY: Where do you get off trying to …

TRACEY: Where I get off is none of your stupid business.

JAY: You're hanging around my house at night.

TRACEY: I don't know what you're talking about.

JAY: What? You think I'm stupid.

TRACEY: As a matter of fact …

JAY: You think I don't have eyes in my head? Even my mum's seen you. Last night she's doing the dishes and she calls my dad over to come look at that girl again.

TRACEY: I was going to the store.

JAY: Right. Every single night you go to the store …

TRACEY: I ran out of smokes …

JAY: What the hell is it you want from me?

TRACEY: Nothing.

JAY: I've had it with your bullshit. I mean it Tracey ...

TRACEY: You're just pissed off because Katie dumped you, a mental case dumped you ...

JAY: This isn't about Katie, this about you and me.

TRACEY: You and me. See? Something did happen.

JAY: What?

TRACEY: Something happened between you and me ...

JAY: Last summer? Ah, Christ. Nothing happened.

TRACEY: Yes it did. We we did something.

JAY: We slept together.

TRACEY: We ...

JAY: Don't try and tell me I'm the first guy ... Just forget it, Tracey. Keep away from me. You hear?

JAY begins to walk away. JORDAN enters. TRACEY and JAY don't notice him.

You know something else? I never even wanted to fool around with you. Ever. Shit. It would've been a lot less hassle to have just gone off on my own with a magazine. Keep out of my way, Tracey. Back off!

JAY exits. JORDAN approaches TRACEY, reaches out to comfort her.

TRACEY: Don't.

Scene 16

BELLA and KATIE in the washroom.

BELLA: Know what I just heard? "Fatty fatty, two by four, can't get through, the bathroom door." How original. I haven't heard that one since grade two.

KATIE: Don't let it get to you.

BELLA: Fat people are deaf. Stupid too. Fat people never really get hurt. They're jolly.

BELLA takes her Thigh Master out of her pack.

My goal is the Valentine's Dance.

KATIE: Maybe it would be easier if you could just accept …

BELLA: Look, Katie, I *am* fat. It's not like you. You look in the mirror and think you're fat but it's nonsense. I've always been big. And I've always wanted to be little. End of story.

KATIE: (*looking in mirror*) Look. Look at yourself.

BELLA: No.

KATIE: It's an exercise we do in group.

BELLA: On New Year's Eve I added it all up. I've lost and gained and lost and gained and lost and gained sixty pounds this year.

KATIE: These are my hands—long and narrow like my mother's.

BELLA: All those little girls, those stupid little girls. In kindergarten they get to sit in the front row and hand everything out. They sit in these cute little baby desks. They get away with stuff.

TRACEY enters.

They still do.

KATIE: These are my legs, long like my dad's—big long feet like his too. I used to want a straight line that went from here to here. (*outlining her hips*) But these are my hips, wide, strong. My body is doing exactly what it's supposed to.

BELLA: Mine isn't. Everything's out of control.

KATIE: It's not an "it" Bella. Your body is just a part of you.

BELLA: (*showing a magazine to KATIE*) This is what they call full-figured. She's five-foot-ten and weighs twenty-two pounds less than me. My chest was that big in grade six. What do they expect? I can't do this anymore, I really can't.

KATIE takes BELLA 's hand and touches BELLA's face with it.

KATIE: This is my face—soft, pretty ...

TRACEY: Stupid.

KATIE: Pardon me?

TRACEY: You're both so stupid.

KATIE: Some kids were just teasing Bella about being overweight ...

TRACEY: What if you looked alright? What if the way you looked was the only good thing about you?

KATIE: This is my head, my heart ...

TRACEY: What if you knew exactly how great you looked in tight jeans and it didn't matter ...

KATIE: These are my arms, another vital part of me ...

TRACEY: What if you couldn't have what you wanted? Not ever.

Scene 17

JAY and KATIE are in the Science classroom. They are dissecting a rat, studying for a quiz.

JAY: How come you weren't at the Valentine's Dance?

KATIE: I had to study.

JAY: Jimbo Williams and I had a twenty-sixer of rum. Well, mostly rum—there was some beer mixed in with it too. He had his dad's car. It was great.

KATIE: This must be the esophagus ...

JAY: I looked for you. I kept thinking you'd come.

KATIE: (*reading from lab book*) The striated muscle of the proximal esophageal body is flaccid at rest.

JAY: Flaccid. I thought you said it was a girl ...

KATIE: God! Don't you ever worry about marks?

JAY: I worry about some things ...

KATIE: And drinking and driving, by the way, is extremely dumb.

JAY: I didn't.

KATIE: Good.

JAY: Jimbo did. Why wouldn't you let me see you in the hospital?

KATIE: (*referring to book*) Name the three types of stomachs ...

JAY: I came every day for a week.

KATIE: Simple, complex and ... and ... and ... the kind with the gizzard.

JAY: Give the lady a prize.

KATIE: You ask me something.

JAY: Alright. It's a tough one. It's hard to even ask. Are you going out with someone?

KATIE: We've got a quiz in ten minutes. C'mon.

JAY: When you were in the hospital I thought I could just pick you up and carry you home like that time you fainted.

KATIE: Name the parts of the digestive tract in humans.

JAY: You're not even listening.

KATIE: Yes I am and I can take care of myself, thank you very much. I talked to Mr. Simmons. I want a new lab partner. I can't stand this. I mean it. I'm not going to fail because of you ...

JAY: You asked for a new partner?

KATIE: I've been asking for a new partner since September. The act of swallowing. What's it called?

JAY: It's called bullshit.

KATIE: Deglutition ... Describe the first phase ... Jay? Describe all three phases.

JAY: The first phase is standing up for someone when the whole school just thinks she's a stuck-up bitch.

The second phase is getting totally hung up on her and getting very concerned when she gets sick. (*gathering up his books to exit*) Wanna know the third phase Katie? Wanna know how it all ends?

KATIE: In the first phase the food is directed into the back of the mouth ...

JAY: In the last phase the guy who has been basically decent to the girl finally tells the bitch to go fuck herself.

JAY exits. KATIE takes out another notebook and begins writing to her dad.

KATIE: Dear Dad: Things here are super! Enclosed please find a copy of my second-term report card. I, too, am disappointed by the *B* in Science but, as you know, this is because of my partner; it has absolutely nothing to do with me.

Scene 18

TRACEY and JORDAN are at their lockers.

TRACEY: Five bucks.

JORDAN: Ten.

TRACEY: Seven-fifty. Once a week.

JORDAN: Seven-fifty but only in the parking lot. The school parking lot.

TRACEY: The whole school's gonna watch *you* teach *me* how to drive?

JORDAN: Those are the terms. Take them or leave them. And I only get the car for special occasions. Dentist appointments, field trips. That sort of thing. So don't go bugging me for more time.

TRACEY: Just tell your dad you're in the choir or the chess club. Tell him you're swamped with after-school *dork* activities.

JORDAN: This is great. I'll teach you how to drive and you'll teach me how to lie.

TRACEY: We have a deal?

JORDAN: (*pause*) I don't know ...

TRACEY: Jordan!

TRACEY gives him a little kiss on the cheek.

JORDAN: Deal.

TRACEY exits. JORDAN remains at his locker.

Scene 19

KATIE is finishing off her letter in the Science room.

KATIE: I finish off my History project in a few weeks. Mum says you have a surprise and that you have to tell us personally. Well. A little bird told me you might come out to visit us at spring break. Please, please let this be true. Everyone sends their love, mum included. I can't wait to see you. Love, love Katie.

Lights go down on KATIE and come up on JORDAN at his locker.

JORDAN: I am completely *utterly* aware of the fact that she kissed me because she wanted a favour. Or perhaps she was just acknowledging that we are, contrary to popular belief, very good friends. I know she doesn't think of me *that way*. But nevertheless I think her kissing me does have a certain significance. Although it was just a kiss on the cheek it was still kind of longish, as if to say, hey ... maybe ... *Why not!*

JORDAN sucks in his gut and puffs out his chest.

Looking good buddy. Looking very good!

Scene 20

Girls' washroom. BELLA is eating her lunch. TRACEY
enters and kicks the garbage can.

BELLA: What's with you?

TRACEY: That stupid *K* car. *K* as in crap.

BELLA: This whole place has been in a bad mood for
a month.

TRACEY: *K* as in completely uncool. Lesson number
· three and Jordan still won't let me out of the
parking lot. If I go more than two miles an hour
he throws a fit. A *K* car—Christ. We look like
undercover cops.

KATIE enters.

BELLA: Hi.

TRACEY: I have to have my license by spring break.
Megadeth's playing Portland. Having my license is
an absolute necessity.

BELLA: Katie? What're you doing for break?

KATIE: Studying.

BELLA: Is your dad coming out?

KATIE: No.

KATIE throws her lunch in the trash.

BELLA: We're going to Disneyland. Can you believe it? I've wanted to go since I was two but not now. You want some chips?

KATIE shakes her head.

TRACEY: I thought you said your mum and dad were getting back together.

KATIE: No I never ...

TRACEY: I did that too when my parents split, thought my dad would come back home. Then, then I used to pretend my whole family just froze to death and drifted away on a glacier and I was the only one left. And for the first time, everything was quiet, no fighting, no nothing.

BELLA: That's demented.

TRACEY: No it isn't. My mum's therapist said those kind of thoughts are completely normal. How's therapy, Katie?

KATIE: I don't have to go anymore.

TRACEY: Therapists, by the way, are totally nuts about me. You know why?

KATIE: I couldn't imagine ...

TRACEY: (*yelling loudly, right into KATIE'S face*) Aaaaaaggghhhh!!!! I'm very in touch with my anger. Shrinks love that kind of crap ...

KATIE: Let me make one thing perfectly clear. My family or me, we're nothing like you.

TRACEY: Is that a fact?

BELLA: Katie we've got class, P.E. ...

KATIE: I'm nothing like either of you. And, Bella, if you really want to feel good about yourself you might try not stuffing your face day in and day out ...

BELLA: But you said ...

KATIE: You know, having a little control in your life isn't a bad thing. It's part of our nature.

TRACEY: She's not eating.

BELLA: I don't stuff my face. I put on weight easily, I always have.

KATIE: Excuse me but you just had one sandwich, one orange, two very large cookies and an assortment of noodle things in those Tupperware bowls, a Diet Coke and a bag—a twenty percent extra—bag of chips.

TRACEY: Yeah? What'd you have Katie?

KATIE: Some apple.

TRACEY: An apple a day keeps the doctor away ... I've been watching you. You're not eating. All that stuff about being better? It's just talk ...

KATIE: Jay's right about you—you're always sticking your nose in where it doesn't belong.

TRACEY: Jay! I have not gone near him in ages ... You *quit* your group. Am I right?

KATIE: You don't know me. And I don't want *anything* to do with either of you!

KATIE exits. BELLA calls out after her.

BELLA: I can't help it!

TRACEY: It's okay, Bella.

BELLA: I don't have any control.

TRACEY: I thought my first time would be like that. We'd be so in love we'd be completely out of control. I wanted my first time to be like that ... Correction. My first time *was* like that. Shit. He's such a liar. Bella? You're fine.

Scene 21

BELLA is walking down the hall. She has been crying.
JORDAN spots her.

BELLA: Do you have any chips?

JORDAN: No ... Bella, you okay?

BELLA: Fine. Don't look at me.

JORDAN: No you're not. What's wrong?

BELLA: I need some chips. An economy size two-bag box of chips.

JORDAN: Tracey ... Has she been bugging you, hurting your ...

BELLA: Not her. Katie.

JORDAN: Katie ...

BELLA: Sometimes she can be incredibly mean. Everyone can be incredibly mean ...

JORDAN: Tell me about it. Tracey just kicked the fender on my dad's car. She scratched it. I'm not kidding.

BELLA: If I had no one to go with and you had no one to go with ...

JORDAN: Where?

BELLA: To grad.

JORDAN: Grad's two years away.

BELLA: If neither of us had anyone to go with ...
could we ... could we go together?

JORDAN: Sure. But that's way in the future, Bella.
You'll probably be married by then, a good Italian
girl like you ...

BELLA: You mean it? You'll really go with me? I get so
worried I'll miss it. I get so worried I can't sleep at
night. You really mean it?

JORDAN: Bella I'd *like* to go with you. Even if you're
going out with someone I'll hold you to it. I'll *force*
you to go with me. It's a date and I'm it. Okay?

BELLA: Deal.

Scene 22

TRACEY yells down the hall at JAY.

TRACEY: Hey, *asshole!* Yeah you, *Jay!* I'm talking to you.

JAY: Not so loud ...

TRACEY: You had *no right* to talk to me that way.

JAY: What? When?

TRACEY: Last month ...

JAY: Let's just forget it, okay?

TRACEY: And stop telling me I'm *pretending* something
happened last summer. Something *did happen.* And
it wasn't just once and you damn well know it. You
know I really liked you. I told you I loved you. So
you're the one that can stop pretending,
pretending we just had some one-night stand.

JAY: Okay. Just keep it down ...

TRACEY: And I don't care what you do now. You can
go run off with eight million girls or with Katie ...

JAY: I'm not going to ...

TRACEY: Just don't ever, *ever* tell me again how I'm
supposed to feel because at least I had the guts to
be honest with you.

TRACEY begins to exit. JAY calls out after her. Lights also begin to come up on KATIE, by herself in the washroom, shell-shocked, staring at the garbage can.

JAY: Yo! Tracey!

TRACEY: What?

JAY: You've got way more class than Katie.

Scene 23

*In the washroom, lights come up full on KATIE staring
at the trash can. She goes through it frantically,
looking for her lunch. TRACEY enters and watches
KATIE as KATIE scatters bits of garbage and food
wildly throughout the room. KATIE finds her bag, rips
it open and holds her apple like a prize. She notices
TRACEY and she gasps.*

KATIE: Please.

TRACEY: What?

KATIE: Please don't tell. Just leave me alone, just leave
me ...

TRACEY: Did you lose something?

KATIE: Yes.

TRACEY: Something valuable?

KATIE: Yes ...

TRACEY: What?

KATIE: My lunch.

*KATIE carefully quarters her apple and places it on a
piece of paper towel in front of her.*

KATIE: I can eat one quarter but it has to be the
smallest piece. I can't tell which one is the smallest.
Can you?

TRACEY: Why can you only eat one quarter?

KATIE: Because yesterday I ate two and I felt stuffed, gross all day.

TRACEY: You're not gross ...

KATIE: Buying this apple—two for a dollar. I hate that. Everything should be sold by weight or else you can't be exactly sure of what you're getting.

TRACEY: I'll eat this piece and you eat the other. Okay?

KATIE: I'm going to Toronto.

TRACEY: To see your dad? That's great ...

KATIE: There's this dress. I want to wear this dress from two years ago but I'm too big now. I'm too big all across here (*referring to her hips*).

TRACEY: You're *not* big. Just one bite of the apple ...

KATIE: I'm not a bridesmaid but I will be at the front because I *am* family and family's important. Right? Everyone will be watching me ...

TRACEY: Your dad is getting married again? To what's-her-name?

KATIE: I'm very happy for him.

TRACEY: When my mum got remarried I was seven. I tried to throw a rock at her new husband.

KATIE: Andrew and Buddy aren't invited to the wedding; they're too small. Only me.

TRACEY: (*pushing the apple toward her*) Katie, please ...

KATIE: I will not be staying with my dad as he and Cynthia will be needing their privacy. I'm staying with my Auntie Jean ...

TRACEY: Just one bite ...

KATIE: There's these lists, these lists keep growing in me. If I do this and this but not this and don't eat that then maybe he'll come back. But nothing works. Nothing is working. I just hate her so much, my mum. She made him leave.

TRACEY: I thought he was the one that got a girlfriend. In my books I'd tell him to piss off, not her ...

KATIE: I can't.

TRACEY: Well then, I'll be like your teacher. I'm incredibly good at that sort of thing. Piss off. Repeat after me.

KATIE: I don't want to hurt anybody. I keep hurting them and hurting me.

TRACEY: Then just take one bite of this incredibly delicious apple. One bite, Katie, please.

KATIE: It hurts.

TRACEY: I know that. I really do. It's the worst. Absolutely.

TRACEY comforts KATIE. Eventually KATIE reaches for the apple. She eats one quarter then reaches for another.

Scene 24

A slide comes up of a concentration-camp victim from World War II again, as in Scene 4. KATIE finishes delivering her project to her History class: JORDAN, BELLA and JAY. Light remains on TRACEY in the washroom, at the mirror, drying her face.

KATIE: … While at Treblinka the Jews were given nine hundred calories a day. This is the amount scientifically determined to be the minimum necessary to sustain human functioning. For those of you familiar with the Beverly Hills Diet, this is an identical amount.

The effects of involuntary semi-starvation are as follows: irritability, poor concentration, anxiety, depression, apathy, abrupt swings of mood, fatigue and social isolation. All the World War II victims of starvation experienced terrible feelings of guilt over having done something bad for which they were now being punished … (*she stops for a moment, then to herself*) But it wasn't … It wasn't their fault … (*reads again*) They dreamed of every kind of food in limitless amounts. Even years later, when they were safe and sound, they would continue to smuggle and hide food.